CONCEITFUL THOUGHT

*The Interpretation
of English
Renaissance
Poems*

ALASTAIR FOWLER

AT THE UNIVERSITY PRESS
EDINBURGH

*

© Alastair Fowler 1975
Edinburgh University Press
ISBN 85224 286 7
Printed in Great Britain

Contents

Preface p. vii

*

Also by Alastair Fowler

CRITICISM

Spenser and the Numbers of Time
(Routledge 1964)
Triumphal Forms
(Cambridge University Press 1970)

EDITIONS

R. Wills *De re poetica*
(Blackwell 1958)
J. Milton *Paradise Lost*
(Longman 1968)
C. S. Lewis *Spenser's Images of Life*
(Cambridge University Press 1967)
Silent Poetry
(Routledge 1970)
Topics in Criticism
(with Christopher Butler:
Longman 1971)

*

Conceitful
Thought

Preface

The six essays making up this book are about Renaissance poems that seem to me to lie, for one reason or another, on the confines of criticism. I mean by this that the poems, though well known and provisionally at least valued, have not been easy to approach critically, but like many in their period have needed an unexpected amount of preliminary exploration by interpretative methods. Not that they have always received scholarly attention of the requisite sort. Indeed, what sets a limit to our critical understanding in this direction is precisely that interpretative problems are eluctable, even missed altogether. Sixteenth-century language is already close enough to our own to give the illusion of being readable without translation. And poems in the style C. S. Lewis called golden may seem not to need explanation. I become more and more convinced, however, that Tudor poetry may really be quite difficult to interpret with any degree of precision, in spite of an appearance of straightforwardness if not mere simplicity.

Each chapter attempts to scout a different hermeneutic barrier. With Wyatt the problems are of remote sentiments and social conventions. The chapter on Surrey touches a more textural difficulty arising when rhetorical schemes or structural patterns become obscure. Sidney's *Ye goatherd gods* serves as a paradigmatic instance of a poem whose unsuspected complexities baffle by the simplicity of their pastoral disguise. Many Elizabethan poems have a far greater occasional element than is often realized: *Prothalamion* exemplifies this feature, as well as the recursive or self-referring devices characteristic of mannerist poetry. Another chapter, more discursive, argues that the Spenserian (or Shakespearean) conceit has suffered by being regarded as 'easy' by comparison with the Metaphysical conceit. And finally *To Penshurst* shows the elusiveness of both tone and topicality in a poem of patronage, together with complications of genre. Naturally all or many of these problems may arise with a single poem; but I have tried to take pronounced instances, which might have theoretical interest. For the same reason I have sometimes pressed the analysis *ad extremum*, to the point where speculation begins to pass probability.

vii

I make no apology in this regard, since it is precisely the need to consider the limits of intention afresh that I mean to draw attention to. At the same time, I should emphasize that these are not critical, but descriptive or interpretative essays. They deal with preliminary questions of a sort anyone will have to answer before adequate criticism or critical history can be written.

None of the essays has been published before except the last, which appeared in a somewhat different form as 'The "Better Marks" of Jonson's *To Penshurst*', in *The Review of English Studies* n.s. 24 (1973). However, parts of most of the others have been included in lectures and informal talks, so that many contributions and corrections deserve acknowledgement—so many that the debts must be consolidated here. Special thanks, however, are due to Dr John North of the Museum of the History of Science, Oxford, whose frequent advice and help with calculations made possible the astronomical parts of chapter 4. It should be added, to save the phenomena, that the remaining errors are mine. Professors Angus McIntosh and Eric J. Dobson gave generous and valuable help with some difficult words, and Miss E. M. Brown commented very helpfully on chapter 5.

I am much indebted to Miss A. S. Wheelaghan, Mrs A. West, Miss S. E. Strathdee and Miss J. Strobridge, secretaries in the Department of English Literature at the University of Edinburgh, who typed the final version of the MS.

In quotations I have modernized spelling (except for proper names), but retained original punctuation. Where editorial pointing has had to be introduced (in certain MS texts) this has been indicated. The modern system of punctuation by no means corresponds, even after change of symbols, to the Tudor system. Moreover, old punctuation sometimes contains valuable evidence of intention as to phrasing and rhythm. For example, the Egerton MS text of *Who so list to hunt* (p. 2 below) is so heavily pointed as to give the impression of a specially prepared reading script. In references, the place of publication is omitted if it is London.

A. D. S. F.
University of Edinburgh

I

Obscurity of Sentiment in
the Poetry of Wyatt

Thomas Wyatt's reputation as a poet surprises by its instability. It swings wildly in comparison with the gently declining esteem that Surrey has continued, justly or not, to engage. In the eighteenth century, Wyatt was not even preferred. And our own century's best estimates of his work, and of the relative importance of its parts, have differed sharply. To E. M. W. Tillyard the songs represent the highest achievement, to H. A. Mason the psalms. And Patricia Thomson's recognition of 'genius'[1] would be hard to reconcile with C. S. Lewis's restrictive judgement—'For those who like their poetry lean and sinewy and a little sad . . . a capital poet'.[2] In part this situation can be attributed on the one hand, to the difficulty of associating Wyatt with Continental and Neo-Latin literary contexts, on the other to those problems of text and canon to which Mason has recently recalled our straying attention. All the same, the disparities remain puzzling —until you notice that critics who discuss individual Wyatt poems differ equally sharply in their interpretations. Wyatt's meaning often appears not to be well understood.

True, his diction seems simple: it noticeably avoids aureate forms and International Gothic Latinisms.[3] Simple as their language seems, however, Wyatt's poems can be misinterpreted. Does this happen, perhaps, just because of their colloquial directness—since we ourselves are now so far from belonging to the immediate audience? A reticence that Wyatt's poetry holds is one met in much Tudor court poetry: namely, social privacy:

> if we could enter their world and see their lyrics as gambits in a 'game of love', half-mocking, half-serious, we might then be less puzzled by them. The smooth impersonality of the courtly lyric

[1] *Sir Thomas Wyatt and His Background* (1964) 200.
[2] *English Literature in the Sixteenth Century Excluding Drama* (Oxford 1954) 230.
[3] See Thomson 130, R. Southall *The Courtly Maker* (Oxford 1964) 22.

may easily deceive us. The shades and nuances of meaning—everything, in fact, that might distinguish the individual from the type—arose from situation, not from words.[4]

Raymond Southall has given a convincing account of the Devonshire MS, which may serve as a paradigm of one sort of circulated collection.[5] It seems that when borrowers returned the manuscript they would add contributions, together sometimes with a cryptically brief personal message. Thus the poems served as social communications; they not only alluded to, but might factitively constitute, shared intimacies. So far as possible from anonymity, they could take for granted a common intimacy of whose existence we are usually denied even external knowledge. Ignorant of this biographical context, we should not be surprised to find the horizon of meaning uncomfortably wide.

"Who so List to Hunt".

This is true even with a relatively public poem such as *Who so list to hunt*, which tradition not implausibly connects with Wyatt's own courtly love for Anne Boleyn:

Who so list to hunt: I know where is an hind,
    But as for me: helas; I may no more.
    The vain travail hath wearied me so sore.
    I am of them, that farthest cometh behind.
Yet, may I, by no means, my wearied mind
    Draw from the deer: but as she fleeth afore
    Fainting I follow. I leave off therefore:
    Sithens in a net I seek to hold the wind.
Who list her hunt: I put him out of doubt:
    As well, as I: may spend his time in vain.
    And, graven with diamonds, in letters plain:
There is written, her fair neck round about:
    Noli me tangere: for Caesar's I am:
    And wild for to hold: though I seem tame.
        (Egerton MS 2711)

Commentators disagree even about the poem's drift. Some share Patricia Thomson's view that 'the sentiment is arrogant and cynical.

---

[4] J. Stevens *Music and Poetry in the Early Tudor Court* (1961) 208; but cf. Southall 174.
[5] On another sort of MS collection see L. G. Black *Studies in Some Related Manuscript Poetic Miscellanies of the 1580s* Oxford D. Phil. Thesis 1970.

To describe the pursuit of an inaccessible lady as so much time spent "in vain" is to aim a blow at the foundation of the sentiment of courtly love common to Petrarch and the Petrarchans.[6] But Raymond Southall (p. 89) finds not a trace of cynicism: for him Wyatt 'plainly brings to his work the standards and demands of real affection.' The critics seem at times to be discussing different poems. And behind these diverse constructions we detect different biographical assumptions. Southall, assuming Caesar's 'proprietary rights' to be Henry 8's, imagines Wyatt condemning Anne Boleyn's *amour courtois* as a frivolous 'hypocritical game': Patricia Thomson, in a way more cautious, thinks that the poem 'may refer to Henry 8's appropriation of Anne Boleyn' but is sure that 'at any rate it describes the loss of a mistress to some lordly husband or master, and the consequent futility, even danger, of pursuing her further' (p. 199); also that it treats 'the pursuit of what is obviously a wayward court lady' (p. 197). Both formulations, as we shall see, involve false biographical constructions.

Interpretation has been obfuscated by confusion about genre. Critics used to treat *Who so list to hunt* as an imitation of Petrarch's *Una candida cerva* (*Rime* 190), so that its sentiments were classed as Petrarchan or un-Petrarchan. Thus, the original told of the lover's pathetic grief at the disappearance of a visionary hind, symbolizing Laura's liberation from mortal life; whereas the English imitation treated a more mundane, tougher and altogether un-Petrarchan sort of wild freedom. Again, there was controversy as to whether Romanello's *Una cerva gentil* also influenced Wyatt. Then Patricia Thomson, from the vantage of fuller learning, saw that the matter was less simple. Out of any of a shoal of Petrarchan commentators Wyatt could have gathered information about such matters as the legend that NOLI ME TANGERE QUIA CAESARIS SUM was a motto inscribed on the collars of Caesar's free-ranging deer.[7] Now the interpreter's questions had to become more sophisticated: he must ask whether Wyatt was authorized by the commentaries to use this meaning, obligated by them not to use that other. For example, he had to know that it was within the tradition to interpret Caesar's

[6] p. 197; cf. H. A. Mason *Humanism and Poetry in the Early Tudor Period* (1959) 188, J. W. Lever *The Elizabethan Love Sonnet* (1956) 25.
[7] See K. Muir and P. Thomson (eds) *Collected Poems of Sir Thomas Wyatt* (Liverpool 1969) 267. M. Praz *Studies in Seventeenth-Century Imagery* (Rome 1964) 13 discusses a heraldic application, Lucrezia Gonzaga's *impresa* of a white doe with the motto NESSUN MI TOCCHI, described by Ruscelli and Pittoni.

freeing of the hind in a worldly sense, as a reference to Laura's marriage: 'per Cesare intendono la maritale legge da Cesare ordinata, per laquale dee esser solo del suo marito e d'ogni altra persona libera si, che nessuno molesto esser le debba' (Gesualdo).[8] The same commentator could give Wyatt grounds for stressing a hunting metaphor only implicit in Petrarch. And it became a duty for a modern critic to note that 'the wild seeming-tame lady owes nothing to either Petrarch or the commentators'.[9] Engaging though this play of thought has been, it misconceives the nature of imitation and the generic pressures it exerts.

For one thing, Petrarch and his commentators need not have been Wyatt's only sources of information about the ghostly hind, sometimes sacred to Diana, which materializes in such authorities as Pliny, Plutarch, Valerius Maximus and Solinus.[10] The sixteenth-century historian Guagninus not only attaches Solinus' marvel to the modern King Charles 6, but actually mentions the use of nets—compare 'sithens in a net'—in her hunt.[11] Besides, even if *Who so list to hunt* belongs to a love-complaint sub-genre with a Petrarchan tradition, Wyatt was free to modify its individual types. He could use or ignore its forms, to make a distinct work in neither obedience nor reaction to Petrarch. What matters is the poetic use to which Wyatt puts his material and his forms, whether Petrarchan or other.

Who so list to hunt uses a conceit from the chase to amplify despair at failure. The hunter-lover's 'vain' effort tires him so much that he lags among the last; but in spite of exhaustion and 'fainting' he cannot at first draw himself away. What is this but a tribute to the deer–dear quarry's irresistible attraction? Even when the lover finally abandons the hunt, it is not because he feels the hind any less desirable, but because he has lost all hope of success. This is expressed in a proverbial form—'in a net I seek to hold the wind'[12]—whose aptness has

---

[8] cit. Thomson 199. [9] ibid. 198.

[10] Pliny *Hist. nat.* 8.50; Plutarch *Life of Sertorius* 11.3–4; Valerius Maximus *Memorabilia* 1.2; Solinus *Collectanea* ed. Mommsen (1895) 107. On the availability of Plutarch's *Lives* see D. A. Russell *Plutarch* (1973) 147–8.

[11] *Hist. Franc.* 9.3: 'in casses et retia compellit. Erat in torque literis latinis inscriptum: HOC ME CAESAR DONAVIT'; cit. Giosuè Carducci et al. (eds) *Francesco Petrarca: Le Rime* (Florence 1957) 275.

[12] *A Dictionary of the Proverbs in England in the Sixteenth and Seventeenth Centuries* ed. M. P. Tilley (Ann Arbor, Mich. 1950) W 416 and *The Oxford Dictionary of English Proverbs* ed. F. P. Wilson (Oxford 1970) 111, citing Erasmus *Adagia*, Lyly *Midas* 5.1.24 'As impossible . . . as to catch the wind in a net', etc.

been said to depend on the familiarity of nets or webs as metaphors for amorous strategies in pursuits of the heart.[13] The proverb itself implied the futility of the attempt rather than the inconstancy of the wind: Petrarch, indeed, applied it to a lady of '*rigida alma*'.[14] Yet the lover is far from any cynical (or for that matter austere) questioning of the value of erotic venery. On that topic he has nothing directly to say. Nor is arrogance anywhere to be discovered: he compares himself rather unfavourably with the rest of the field. On the other hand, *pace* Southall, the sonnet by no means criticizes the hind. Indeed, its sestet insists on despair in a most complimentary way. All huntsmen will be as unsuccessful as the speaker.

The hind's collar displays her chaste nature emblematically, dissuading huntsmen by its inscription 'graven with diamonds'. Now, the diamonds and topazes of Laura's collar stood for constancy and chastity: 'ferma constantia contra ogni ribolliment lascivo', according to the commentator Vellutello. And in the iconological language of gems in Wyatt's time, the faithfulness of the diamond was almost a *cliché*.[15] More than a century later, Dryden understood the implication of 'solid crystal;/ Seen through, but never pierced' (*All for Love* 4.202–3). Diamonds are, as we can still say, forever. In objection, nothing can be made of the point that whereas Petrarch has 'scritto . . . di diamanti' Wyatt has 'graven' (as if the diamond firmness were Caesar's, in the graving tool, not the hind's, on the collar); for Hawes could equate the two formulations in a description of similar collar legends.[16] In such contexts *graven* often meant 'impressed deeply: fixed indelibly'.[17] Besides, even if the hind's collar contained no diamonds, its inscription would remain perdurable.

Another way to find room for cynical irony is to take the hard warning of ownership as a Caesarian injunction only, belied by the

---

[13] e.g. Chaucer *Troilus* 3.1353–5, where eyes are 'Ye humble nettes of my lady deere'.
[14] *Canzoniere* 239.37–9: 'In rete accolgo l'aura e 'n ghiaccio i fiori,/ E 'n versi tento sorda e rigida alma/ Che né forza d' Amor prezza né note'.
[15] G. de Tervarent *Attributs et symboles dans l'art profane 1450–1600* (Geneva 1958 and 1964) col. 148 cites heraldic devices, diamonds with the mottos BONA FIDE, A LA BONNE FOI, SINE FRAUDE.
[16] S. Hawes *The pastime of pleasure* 169–72: 'Theyr colers were of golde   and of tyssue fyne/ Wherin theyr names   appered by scypture/ Of dyamondes   that clerely do shyne/ The lettres were graven fayre and pure'.
[17] *OED* s.v. *Grave* v.[1] III 6 b, e.g. (1559) 'Faith in our hearts set and grave'.

hind's actual waywardness. However 'Caesar's I am' and 'wild for to hold' are parts of the same inscription: if Caesar graved one, he graved the other. Alternatively, if we take the inscriptions as iconological labels, then we must still allow them compatibility on that level. Thus, the sole reason for suspecting ironic discrepancy lies in the hind's wildness. But this is no reason; for to take *wild* in an unfavourable sense ('wayward', 'licentious') runs counter to the metaphor not only of this poem but of its generic type. In such contexts, wildness means chastity and tameness submission to a lover's will. Think of Wyatt's own *They flee from me*, where tameness—'I have seen them gentle tame and meek/ that now are wild and do not remember'— involves the woman's putting herself 'in danger' by a bedroom visit.[18] The metaphor did not wrest *wild* far from its normal connotation, the common notion being shyness:

> She is too disdainful;
> I know her spirits are as coy [reserved] and wild
> As haggards of the rock.[19]

We conclude that *Who so list to hunt*, far from conveying moral criticism of the hind's lightness, means almost the reverse. As the collar legend states, despite a surface appearance of tameness (approachability) the hind is really chaste ('wild') and faithful to Caesar. If Wyatt's lover blames her for anything, it is for her constancy. The poem may express less obvious despairs and disillusionments too. But it would not be wrong to take it as complimentary to the hind, reassuring to Caesar, expressive of a hopeless admiration. The situation requiring the compliment, perhaps even the degree of tact requisite, may have been known to the first audience.

Uncertainties of Emotional Situation.

Attempts to reconstruct the meaning of early Tudor autobiographical poems may encounter more arduous difficulties. It is not known, for example, whether *Of Carthage he, that worthy warrior* refers to Wyatt's domestic or public life. So we miss the aptness of its economy, or even find it opaque: 'So hangeth in balance/ of war, my peace'. It may be good. Or take the Blage MS *Who list*, a fine poem, perhaps by Wyatt:

---

[18] cf. the carol quoted by R.L. Greene in *Bu R* 12.3 (1964) 22: 'Sum be wyse, and sum be fonde;/ Sum be tame, I understond;/ Sum will take bred at a manus hond'.

[19] *Much Ado* 3.1.34–6; cf. Willobie *Avisa* (1594) ch.47: 'Though coy at first she seem and wild', and *OED* s.v. *Wild* II 6 c.

> The bell tower showed me such sight
> That in my head sticks day and night;
> There did I learn out of a grate,
> For all favour, glory or might,
> That yet *circa regna tonat*.[20]
> (*punctuation editorial*)

The 'sight/ That in my head sticks', whether Anne's beheading or a view of heads on spikes, is perhaps clear enough. Not so the earlier stanza:

> Who list his wealth and ease retain,
> Him self let him unknown contain;
> Press not too fast in at that gate
> Where the return stands by disdain:
> For sure, *circa regna tonat*.

Southall (p.46) supplies biographical context and arrives at advice to lovers: 'if you wish to remain happy and contented you must keep your love to yourself and not thrust yourself into "love's gate", for the reward of service is disdain'. On the same assumption of an erotic-courtly context, one might prefer to paraphrase: 'the reward depends on whims of disdain'—or even 'escape may depend'.[21] On the other hand, perhaps the stanza issues instead a general warning, like those that follow, against overreaching, social climbing 'and blind desire of estate'. Again the first readers may have started from necessary initial assumptions which we only guess at.

Difficult though they can be, these are straightforward problems, which new information or better biographical understanding might in principle enable us to solve. And the difficulty Wyatt already posed in the sixteenth century, when he seems to have been thought obscure and 'too diffuse',[22] is scarcely even troublesome to modern critics who cut their teeth on exegetic ambiguities. But an additional and far more formidable obstacle to interpretation, which may prove absolutely impassable, looms conspicuously in Wyatt's courtly lyrics and others of the same tradition. John Stevens touches the edge of this barrier in the passage quoted earlier. He distinguishes three main classes of courtly lyrics, according to whether they were instruments

[20] Muir and Thomson 187–8.
[21] cf. ibid. 3, 'Return, alas, since thou art not regarded'. Personification and pun are possible: 'where Disdain stands beside the return [angle] of the gate'.
[22] ibid. 215–16: 'My songs were too diffuse,/ They made folk to muse'.

of an actual love; contributions to the social 'game of love'; or dramatizing performances by the poet-as-lover. In all of these, the literary
model differs from our own:

> Shades and nuances of meaning—everything, in fact, that might
> distinguish the individual from the type—arose from situation,
> not from words. The spice and piquancy of debate, the saucy-
> solemn atmosphere of 'problems of love' may have given the
> love-lyric the individuality it so conspicuously lacks when re-
> garded as 'words on the page'. (p. 208)

The situations, we must accept, are sometimes past recall. But suppose they were not. Suppose that we learnt to infer the biographical
context from words, conventions and external evidence. Even then a
farther barrier would remain: namely, the remoteness of the sentiments themselves. It is hard for us to try—so hard that we flinch
from the attempt—to imagine, even with respect to situations far less
alien than these, emotions unfamiliar to us.

Impassable Impassibility.

The diction of courtly lyrics may make us well aware of their unfamiliar emotions: 'Yet this trust I have of full great appearance';
'Too great a proof of true faith presented'; 'Thou hast no faith of him
that hath none'.[23] But even without lexical indications we sometimes
feel a remoteness, as perhaps we ought to always:

> For to love her for her looks lovely
> My heart was set in thought right firmly,
> Trusting by truth to have had redress.
> But she hath made an other promise
> And hath given me leave full honestly.
> Yet do I not rejoyce it greatly
> For on my faith I loved too surely;
> But reason will that I do cease
>   For to love her.
>
> Since that in love the pains been deadly
> Me think it best that readily
> I do return to my first address;
> For at this time too great is the press,
> And perils[24] appear too abundantly
>   For to love her.   (Egerton MS 2711 : *punctuation editorial*)

[23] ibid. 14, 3, 16.   [24] The MS abbreviation could also indicate *parels* (bodies

Here one may understand all the words (*address* = manner of speaking, etc.); grasp something of the dramatic situation (a promise broken, a dismissal like the one in *They flee from me* with its 'I have leave to go of her goodness'); sense the general tenor; and yet remain baffled by the reference to emotions of indeterminate character and incalculable implications. The poem is elusive rather than difficult. We may put individual questions: Why should anyone suppose that it would 'rejoyce' the lover to be given leave? Merely because it set him free? Or because being treated 'honestly' (in one sense) was better than being deceived? How does the sure love of the first stanza accord with the prudence of the second? How could a serious love be switched off, or at least into abeyance 'at this time'? And, if the lady has made another promise, why do a whole band of suitors surround her? But if these particular questions were answered, we might still feel the Sisyphism of the need to imagine further questions, and yet others, before it was possible to think how best to entertain sentiments so foreign.

I have tried not to exaggerate Wyatt's cultural distance. Indeed, *For to love her* is a poem which shows his modernity as well as any: he consciously writes about a particular 'fashion of forsaking'. Elsewhere, as Southall has argued, he shows unusual awareness of the *absurdité* of *amour courtois*. His insertion, in an imitation of *Mirando 'l sol de' begli occhi sereno*, of the additional contrary 'twixt earnest and game' is characteristic: he has come a very long way, for good or ill, from Petrarch.[25] And Stevens's laudable attempt to return the English poet's work to a medieval courtly tradition must fail, to the extent that it neglects the aspects stressed by Mason. Wyatt came after a generation of English Humanism, and several of the Continental Renaissance. His sombre moral vision recognizably belongs to the northern Renaissance, although he is not ignorant of recent Italian literature.[26] Nevertheless, in spite of all these qualifications, when Wyatt's sensibility is carefully apprehended it must seem far from the Elizabethan, let alone the modern world. Sidney's Astrophil says little of the deserts of service, and would not conceivably think it a happy issue to be given 'leave to go'. One wonders whether large shifts of sensibility, movements of tectonic plates of the emotional world, may not have made whole areas of feeling inaccessible. If so,

[25] Muir and Thomson 22.   [26] cf. Southall 37.

of troops), as H. A. Mason *Editing Wyatt* (Cambridge 1972) 15.

when we find ourselves excluded from a literary work, analogical exploration may not serve. To put it in another way, the emotions may no longer be in our repertoire. Was a courtly lover's relief at being given honourable leave *anything* like what a modern lover might feel at the end of an unhappy affair? Perhaps elaborate research could arrive at a probable answer. But not easily. And the laboriousness of establishing a basis for empathy militates against effective synthesis. At such junctures we have intimations of an impassable hermeneutic divide. It is not only easier to misread; it is almost more effective.

Here we approach theoretical issues of a universal character. Indeed, John Douglas Boyd has used Wyatt's *There was never nothing more me pained* to illustrate the irreconcilable subjectivism of literary interpretations.[27] To invent a hypothetical seven, all supposedly 'convincing to some degree' yet differing 'in fundamental ways', is his tactic. Divergence is inevitable, because the human experience imitated is itself subject to differently structured viewpoints. Boyd's interpretations have been described as intellectually implausible, since, for example, the refrain line 'Alas the while', which his straw critics attribute now to this speaker now to that, is simply a refrain.[28] But reducing Boyd's argument by piecemeal refutation hardly meets its theoretical challenge. The challenge is to the determinacy of meaning, on the ground that emotions have no objective content. Wyatt's poem belongs to a dramatic lyric genre in which emotions undoubtedly play strong parts. But that may not be the only reason why Boyd found it convenient to choose. We find difficulty in synthesizing its attitudes not just because they involve subjective emotions, but because they involve unfamiliar subjective emotions. In this regard all Boyd's interpretations, whether ironic or not, suffer from a similar defect, that of dealing in modern, or simply counter-modern, emotional conceptions. The best is one that supposes some fault of love on the lover's part, occasioning an unironic compunction at his mistress' regret 'that ever she me loved'. But Boyd takes for granted biographical implications that should properly be explored at an early stage of reconstruction. What situation do the lines 'That ever she me loved' and 'On him that loveth not me' imply? The lover can hardly have rejected his mistress altogether, since he calls her 'my sweet heart'. Was his love deficient? Unfaithful? Light? Are we to conjecture the fault at all, or to concentrate exclusively on the compunction?

[27] *EC* 21 (1971) 327–46.
[28] So J. Daalder in *EC* 21 (1971) 418–24.

While Boyd's hypothetical interpretations are easily disposed of, theoretical scruples linger. And we wonder whether divergent yet simultaneously plausible constructions of fictional emotions have not in fact been made, in connection with other poems if not with this.

Just that seems to be true of Wyatt's *They flee from me.*

The Case of "They Flee from Me".

This admired poem has become the covert for an interminable hunt, which has checked at thickets of erudition or run through open speculation, without an agreed death. The critical literature is so extensive that commentators now feel obliged to apologize for adding to the obstinate poem's *peine forte et dure.*[29]

> They flee from me that sometime did me seek
>   With naked foot stalking in my chamber.
> I have seen them gentle tame and meek
>   That now are wild and do not remember
> That sometime they put themself in danger
>   To take bread at my hand: and now they range
>   Busily seeking with a continual change.
>
> Thanked be fortune it hath been otherwise
>   Twenty times better; but once in special
> In thin array after a pleasant guise,
>   When her loose gown from her shoulders did fall,
> And she me caught in her arms long and small:
>   Therewithall sweetly did me kiss
>   And softly said Dear heart how like you this?
>
> It was no dream: I lay broad waking.
>   But all is turned thorough my gentleness
> Into a strange fashion of forsaking;
>   And I have leave to go of her goodness,
> And she also to use new fangleness.
>   But since that I so kindly am served
>   I would fain know what she hath deserved.
>
>   (Egerton MS 2711: *punctuation editorial*)

R. L. Greene's crisp *Bucknell Review* essay gratefully renders armies of previous commentators redundant, who once disputed whether

---

[29] To the bibliography in Greene 18–20, 23–4, 27–8 add Muir and Thomson 299; C. E. Nelson in *MLR* 58 (1963) 60–3; D. M. Friedman in *SEL* 7 (1967) 1–13; and J. Buxton *A Tradition of Poetry* (1967) 15–17.

II

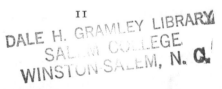

stanza 1 refers to falcons or deer, and whether the lady in stanza 2 is Fortune. Needless now to rehearse their circumstantial evidence: Greene has convinced the academy that Fortune's attributes are conspicuously absent, and that no single animal or bird has characteristics consistent with all the poem's details. Bread is not the food of falcons nor rooms the habitat of deer. Even 'put themselves in danger / To take bread at my hand', is shown to have a close analogue in a satiric carol about women: 'some [women] be tame, I understand; some will take bread at man's hand'. However, although Greene achieves a simplification, he scarcely proves that 'they' refers to women only. He has driven off the falcons and deer, but he has not eliminated the non-specific animal imagery that Donald M. Friedman hypothesizes (pp. 6–8). Indeed, the carol analogue itself uses such imagery; as do several locutions in Wyatt—'tame . . . wild' and 'range . . . seeking'—commonly applied to animals. And Arnold Stein's impression of 'a tension of reference between the animal and the human' has yet to be dispelled.[30] Besides, even if the animal hypothesis were disproved, that would not quite establish plurality of mistresses. There is still the notion that 'she becomes a kind of *they*' through the inconstancy of her desires (p. 32); the plural expressing the lover's incredulity that that same woman could kiss him sweetly and reject him strangely. In much this vein Shakespeare's Troilus exclaims—in variation of the 'Nunc te cognovi' *topos*[31]— —'This is Diomed's Cressida. . . . If there be rule in unity itself,/ This is not she'.

Several interpretations remain unreconciled. In the view of Friedman (pp. 8–11), the first stanza's 'they' implies plural mistresses, thus prejudicing the lover's claim to *gentilezza*; while his dream, a 'sketch of rapacious appetite', offers nothing to suggest devotion or service. Thus an alert reader will see that the final rhetorical ('not genuine') question blames the lady for breaking rules of a game that is 'only a mask for the pursuit of gratification': the speaker himself remains oblivious and 'gravely deceived'. Stein, however, finds the speaker truly gentle: 'the assertion of his gentleness . . . would not be made, we may perhaps assume, if the lady could deny it' (p. 41). The third stanza's uncourtly ironies (such as 'served' in the farm-

[30] *Sew. Rev.* 67 (1959) 33. See *OED* s.v. *Range* v.[1] III 7 a, 'To move hither and thither over a comparatively large area. . . . Sometimes including the idea of searching. . . . Especially of hunting dogs searching for game'.
[31] See B. Otis *Virgil* (Oxford 1964) 104, 115, 119–20.

yard sense[32]) fail to dominate a mainly elegiac expression of personal loss. Stein thinks that the 'noble illusion' of courtly love gets 'knocked about some', but he remains agnostic about how far poet and speaker are conscious of idealization. Most critics have taken 'kindly' as an ironic gibe at the unkind or unnatural behaviour of the lady;[33] but A. S. Gerard sees a reference to the lover's own behaviour—'since I'm served as a man of my kind is likely to be served'. The lover's kind are those bound by gentleness, the code imposing docile obedience to the lady's wishes; so that his conclusion comes out wry but detached, leaving the answer open: 'if the reward of the poet's genuine "gentleness" is desertion, why should not the reward of the lady's (or Fortune's) false "goodness" be company, appreciation and success?' (p. 365). Thus the variety of interpretations proposed with at least some plausibility seems embarassingly rich. The lover is now elegiac and courtly (Stein); now rude and 'quite uncourtly' (J. D. Hainsworth):[34] now courtly though rapacious and self-deceiving (Friedman); now courtly but consciously rebellious, disappointed but wryly detached, frustrated but too mature to philander (Gerard).

Fortunately, all the interpretations can be shown to need radical qualification. For all rest on the assumption that the poem implies a dramatic situation in which a relationship has ended.[35] The sole evidence for this, however, is the words 'but all is turned thorough my gentleness/ into a strange fashion of forsaking' (ll. 16–17). Every commentator has taken 'forsaking' to mean 'abandoning, withdrawing her companionship'; a possible sense suiting the poem's drift.[36] But this was not the only or even perhaps the commonest sense of *forsaking*. Its root notion was 'denial',[37] and a frequent meaning 'decline or refuse something offered'.[38] (In 1605 Camden could still write 'He . . . forsook a right worshipful room when it was offered to him'.) Now this sense suits line 17 admirably. It yields neither elegiac lenity nor 'lovely ritual of euphemism' (Stein 43), but simple

---

[32] Stein 42.

[33] H. Morris sees irony not in *kindly* but in the fact that another, kind lady 'with considerable warmth replaces the former' newfangled lady: *EC* 10 (1960) 485–6. The final line thus becomes speculation—how has the former mistress fared ('been rewarded', a possible sense of *deserved*)? Morris's second mistress is rightly sent packing by A. S. Gerard in *EC* 11 (1961) 362–3.

[34] J. D. Hainsworth *EC* 7 (1957) 94.

[35] e.g. Hainsworth 94; Morris 489; Gerard 363, 365; Friedman 4; Stein 43.

[36] *OED* s.v. *Forsake* v.4, examples from 1300.

[37] ibid. 1, examples from 1250–1511.   [38] ibid. 2, examples from 800–1605.

narration of the speaker's experience: 'all is turned into a distant [strange] manner of refusal of my advances'.[39] Moreover, it aptly continues earlier imagery, turning a former gentle acceptance (of symbolic food) into a refusal.

Several details of the last stanza confirm the conclusion that the lovers' relationship has not, after all, ended. The speaker says 'I have leave to go', not that he has gone. And the lady, though she ranges inconstantly, nevertheless does so by contractual agreement: 'she also [*sc.* 'has leave'] to use newfangleness [practice inconstancy]'.[40] This compact may show weak docility on the speaker's part ('thorough my gentleness'); but that hardly invalidates its mutual permissions. They must continue unless and until he chooses to 'go', that is, to leave the lady's service. That he has not so chosen is a reasonable inference from the interrogative tone of the closure.

A modern reader may suppose that the poem's final question can have only one answer, and therefore implies irony rather than interrogation. But this is to reject the obvious because it affronts our sense of human probabilities. In fact, the final line 'I would fain know what she hath deserved',[41] far from expressing a rhetorical uncertainty, may be urgently existential. Perhaps the speaker really wishes he knew what the lady has deserved of him. Does she deserve farther service? Would a truly gentle lover go or stay? Strange though it seems now, this issue was at one time neither 'uncourtly' nor unreal.

Indeed, it was something of a *demande d'amour*, discussed at length in Andreas Capellanus' *De amore*.[42]

Andreas counsels that if a courtly lover is unfaithful the lady should refuse to receive his love in the future. But then, what if he has candidly asked leave to go, to seek another's embraces ('pro alterius

---

[39] *OED* s.v. *Strange* 11 'Unfriendly; having the feelings alienated; distant or cold in demeanour; reserved; not affable, familiar or encouraging; uncomplying; unwilling to accede to a request or desire'; e.g. *Romeo* 2.2.102: 'I should have been more strange, I must confess'.

[40] *OED* s.v. *Newfangledness* and *Newfangleness*, citing e.g. Chaucer *Anelida and Arcite* 141–13; cf. Chaucer's Balade *Against women unconstant*. Love of novelty.

[41] The form in Egerton MS 2711; cf. the Devonshire MS, B.L. Add. 17492 'What think you by this that she hath deserved?' and Tottel 'How like you this, what hath she now deserved?'

[42] cap. 2.6, 'Si unus amantium alteri fidem frangat amanti': ed. E. Trojel (Munich 1964) 254 ff.; *The Art of Courtly Love* tr. and ed. J.J. Parry (New York 1941) 159 ff.

mulieris amplexibus licentiam ab ipsa precetur')?[43] If she has been so imprudent as to grant such a permission, then she must not 'deny him the regular solaces' until he actually succeeds in taking advantage of it. Now 'the old opinion, held by some'[44] was that all of this applied *pari passu* to the case of the woman's unfaithfulness; although Andreas himself, professing a dual morality, argues that a woman's wantoning with two men should never in any circumstances be condoned. The application to Wyatt's poem is inescapable. An opinion was held that the sort of compact described in stanza 3, though wrong in itself, bound a lover to wait for the outcome before discontinuing relations with his lady. It would be foolish to assume twelfth-century French sentiments in a Tudor poem, although perhaps less foolish than to assume those of twentieth-century Britain. But the courtly code enjoyed a revival in the later Middle Ages, and the popularity of the *De amore* continued into Wyatt's time,[45] so that he and his audience can scarcely have been ignorant of this particular casuistry of gentleness. Thus the poem's final line is probably a courtly and a real question. The lover no doubt suffers and blames; but he also doubts and wavers. Just this may be his double sorrow: to have lost trust and not know whether the loss is final.

To seem to solve an interpretative problem by applying cut and dried lexical or anthropological information is far from my purpose. Lexical confusions perplex *They flee from me*, but only because of the interfretted confusion of unfamiliar emotions. In the absence of knowledge of the appropriate sentimental code, speculations fill the vacuity and misinterpretations abound. We naturally take modern situational types, such as The End of the Affair, for granted. At most, we deprecate the 'idealized' or 'hypocritical' character of courtly love. But although courtly love could be ridiculous, artificial, self-abasing and secretly wanton, it could also be frivolous, crude, orgulously selfish and openly lecherous, or even serious, delicate, generous and chaste. What it almost always was, was variable, elusive, hard to generalize about, and different from anything we feel. Shakespeare's situations often seem strange enough. But between him and Wyatt comes half a

[43] ed. Trojel 259.
[44] 'Antiqua quorundam . . . sententia'; ed. Trojel 260. Thus the present argument does not depend on any particular interpretation of the *De amore* —a relevant point in view of D. W. Robertson's theory of ironic double meaning and homiletic purpose: see *A Preface to Chaucer* (Princeton, N.J. 1963) 393 ff.
[45] Parry 22–4. As many as 12 complete MSS have survived, and there were several printed edns (Strasburg ca 1473, Dortmund 1610, 1614).

century of systematic Reforming effort to extirpate not only the practice of courtly love but even the circulation of romances that might communicate its ideals. For us now to sympathize with the emotions of an early Tudor courtier presents a formidable challenge. At least one critic of Wyatt has appreciated this:

> We can no more imagine the whole of courtly gentleness in all its fresh and complex immediacy, we can no more do this than we can refuse to recognize, under some honoured ancestor's beautiful ceremony of good manners, a kinship of gesture in our own response to social realities. The picture will have faded, the social realities will have changed, whirled through intricate cycles of fashions; but a kind of family likeness can be puzzled out in some lights, especially with the help of other literary pictures, older and newer. . . . We have lost the sure sense of that language [of gentleness] and cannot revive it, but if we recognize the process and see it around us, we can make out some of the words.[46]

The full extent of our loss of the language, however, may never have been appreciated. Now and then we no doubt carry our interpretations of such a poem as *They flee from me* farther. But it is on just those occasions that we sense our general ignorance.

Here the bits of information adduced disclose large new reaches of uncertainty. Does the speaker after all perhaps feel not inconsiderately treated? Would the lady's giving him 'leave to go' be thought a generous fault? And how are we to think of his 'gentleness' as causing her alteration: was he too indulgent or too correct? Something may depend on whether the kiss of fealty described in stanza 2 would have seemed unusually wanton. Commentators have felt it so; but a faultless contemporary heroine enters Squire Meldrum's bedroom, perhaps in much the same circumstances, wearing a 'courlike [elegant] kirtle' that shows 'her paps . . . hard, round, and white'.[47] Again, as to Wyatt's irony, are we now to think of it as directed against the speaker, the lady, or the mode of love? Seeking out a new love has generally been thought more culpable than casually happening on one,[48] so that 'busily seeking' implies some criticism of the lady.[49]

---

[46] Stein 39–40.
[47] Sir D. Lindsay *Squire Meldrum* 933 ff.; ed. J. Kinsley (1959) 47–8. Ovidian sources may be relevant: see C. E. Nelson. Nott and Padelford were surely right to regard the kiss as a courtly kiss of fealty: see A. Berthoff in *Sew. Rev.* 71 (1963) 479 and 482 (dissenting).   [48] cf. Capellanus; tr. Parry 161.
[49] See *OED* s.v. *Busily* 1, 2, 3: curiously, eagerly, energetically.

But even if the poem's main effort amplified the contradictions of love itself, we could not be sure whether it was written against the courtly mode, or simply to express and compose its pains, after the manner of much unrebellious love poetry. Indeed, we know so little of the poem's courtly forms and feelings that we must suppose its real interest to lie elsewhere. Perhaps its underlying situation of un-rewarding commitment happens to be one of enduring interest.

Determinacy of Emotional Terms.

Returning to the theoretical issue raised earlier, we can see that, if the case of *They flee from me* is at all typical, Boyd's argument poses small threat to the determinacy of literary meaning. E. D. Hirsch defends the doctrine of determinacy for the most part in general terms.[50] He provides for subjectivist arguments such as Boyd's only briefly, in the course of establishing reproducibility of meaning against psychologistic objections (pp. 31–40). These he shows to depend on a false equation of meaning with mental processes: that every man's conception of a rainbow is different need not prevent us from understanding the word *rainbow* (p. 32). Hirsch might have to develop his argument to meet the more difficult case of word groups dealing with emotions ('thorough my gentleness'). But he need not reject Boyd's point that the problems of interpreting representations of feeling in Wyatt cannot be resolved 'without an appeal to categories of value much broader than the merely literary' (p. 345). We can admit the subjective 'impurity' of criticism, even the desirability of that condition, and still hope for agreement about verbal meaning. The criticism of *They flee from me* is at a very early stage, yet already certain initial disagreements begin to disappear. We have no reason to suppose its verbal meaning indeterminate, at least in theory.

On the other hand, the case illustrates a different, practical difficulty, of more than local dimensions, for which the doctrine of determinacy scarcely provides. Hirsch's theory provides for the general case of literary works expressing strange states of conscious-ness: the mental process may be alien but the language can in principle always be learnt. Wyatt's poems belong to a special class, however, set apart by the character of the historical tradition through which they have come to us. For literary works may be the best evidence, the best means of acquiring understanding, of outmoded sentimental

[50] *Validity in Interpretation* (New Haven, Conn. 1967) 44–67.

forms. And in the case of courtly love this means of learning the language of emotion is often unavailable. Emotionally obscure poems such as Wyatt's rely heavily on familiarities of experience. Thus the hermeneutic circle becomes viciously tight. We must agree with Hirsch that 'all understanding of cultural entities past or present is "constructed"' (p.43); yet we may doubt whether such construction is possible, where literary texts are themselves the main evidence not only of *sensus* but also of *res*.[51] Many literary works have meanings that must remain, in practice if not in theory, indeterminate.

Wyatt's Modernity.

How then has Wyatt's poetry continued to impress readers? Some would point to its spoken quality. Lewis remarks a 'dramatic quality' (p.230); John Buxton a colloquial force and propensity for 'the natural English prose order of words' (p.12); and Hallett Smith 'a vivid awareness on the poet's part, as he looks back at a poem, that it is spoken and dramatic, and that it takes place in a short time and carries its effects very rapidly'.[52] Maybe Wyatt's vogue has had something to do with our preference for 'poems which talk from the intimacy of a private experience'.[53] But if the popularity of his poems depends on their spoken qualities, it seems all the more remarkable. For it is just the speech rhythms and tones that have suffered time's worst ravages. Significantly, Wyatt's tone has been found debatable in some of his best poems, such as *They flee from me* and *In eternum*. As for his rhythms—not made clearer by the tendency of editors to neglect the pointing of the manuscripts, in spite of its metrical function[54]—they have been involved in controversy for decades, through their repercussions on scansion.

However, there is another more durable element of voice, on which Wyatt seems to have lavished a good deal of attention. I mean the rhetorical conduct: argument, coordinating *concetto*, and what Hallett Smith has called 'general strategy'. In *They flee from me* we sense it in the decisive transitions by which figurative musing (st.1) leads on to a specific memorial narration (st.2) and then to moral questioning. This element proves surprisingly resistant to time.

[51] On the bearing of the distinction between *sensus* and *res* see ibid. 247–8.
[52] *HLQ* 9 (1946) 332.
[53] J. Raban *The Society of the Poem* (1971) 113: 'what we as a society . . . are asking of the poet is that he provide us with "a voice"'.
[54] See Southall 133, Mason *passim*.

Thus we may be in the position of grasping only argumentative force. Or we may sense Wyatt's underlying seriousness without knowing exactly what the seriousness is about. Still, the rhetorical attack may establish a strong position of sincerity: it has a way of unifying resources deployed in its service that produces keen poetic pleasure. This can have communicative precision, even when the emotional referents—*res* and therefore *sensus*—are vague. In consequence, critics who have dwelt on Wyatt's expressive power, or on sentiments such as anti-Petrarchan rebelliousness, may have taken the wrong tack. Even Patricia Thomson, while she rightly discerns typical attitudes in Wyatt's complaints, strays into interrogating their 'sense of betrayal' and judging their idea of 'gentleness' to be 'somewhat barbarous' (p.145). At the present stage of our ignorance feelings expressed in Wyatt's poems are less distinct than obligations cogitated. The obligations are urged with a seriousness of art that comes over, even when we know little of their emotional content. *Barbarous* seems hardly the word to use in connection with such poetry. Of course, ignorance of the feelings does not exempt us from evaluating the obligations. Indeed, Wyatt's poems constantly invite evaluation: constantly there are half-justifications for the theory that his complaints reject the whole absurdity of the courtly love game. Improbable detachment? Perhaps. Yet in a similar way one is also tempted to think of Wyatt as capable of existential nihilism such as one finds in *fin de siècle* or modern complaints.[55]

This is by no means to present Wyatt's poetry as unrepresentative of his own time. To see how far that would be from the truth, one has only to consider the uncertainty of the Wyatt canon. As Southall says (p.25), Wyatt's concerns seem conventional: 'until the poems are allowed to take root in history . . . until the conventions of courtly love are seen to arise out of the need to express the real character of courtly existence', it is difficult to take them as seriously as they deserve. They are so rooted in their society that their survival is incomplete. One may even speak of a failure on Wyatt's part to imagine an audience sufficiently comprehensive, sufficiently free from his own society's presuppositions. But this is to judge by very high standards indeed. And the failure is only partial: Wyatt's detachment, though it falls short of, say, Erasmus', is remarkable enough. After all, the difficulties of his poetry have arisen in part because he attempted

[55] M. Hamburger *The Truth of Poetry* (1969) 51; cf. D.W.Harding in *The Age of Chaucer* ed. B.Ford (Harmondsworth 1954) 206.

forms of communication that were not to be attempted again until after a considerable passage of time and great interruptions of tradition.

These may be thought predictable problems of historical distance. Those we encounter in the poems of Surrey are of a different, more unexpected character.

2

Surrey's
Formal Style

Most critics find the temperate region confusing and prefer to operate
either in the hot zone of poetry as communication (saying) or the
cool zone of poetry as artefact (making). The recently dominant
schools of Formalist criticism appear to have gone in the latter direction. But appearances are a little deceptive. The New Critics, it is
true, left the author and his original audience so much out of account
that they came to treat the work as a fairly simple machine, whose
mechanism could be understood without reference to working pro-
cedures or conventions other than our own. Paradoxically, however,
the Yale critics rebuilt the machine as a direct communication in
current language. Naturally, for this to come off they had to concentrate on a particular canon. In Tudor poetry they wrote about
Wyatt and the Sidney of *Astrophil and Stella* but neglected or disparaged
the *Arcadia*, Spenser and Surrey. Surrey made a specially poor showing: his machines refused to disgorge much ambiguity, irony, or
radical imagery; yet they paid out nothing very interesting in the
way of plain statement either.

Surrey's Simple Logic.

The consequence is a pretty wide agreement that if Surrey has virtues
they are modest ones. Patricia Thomson (pp. 205–6) speaks of his
'harmonious listing' of naturalistic details in *The soot season*, clearly
regarding 'this simplest of structural formulas'—catalogue plus
counterstatement in the manner of Serafino or Cariteo—as rather
puerile. And Lever, who sees only 'an attractive piece of descriptive
verse' (p. 42), contrasts the sonnet somewhat sharply with Petrarch's
mythologically and metaphorically rich *Zephiro torna* (*Canz.* 310). In
the English imitation, spring is simply 'an agreeable natural phenomenon' described in external visual terms that allow neither identification of nature and spirit nor indeed metaphor. As for structure, 'it

is not easy to find even a logical connection between the theme of the poem and the lover's mental state' (pp. 43–4). Now these views seem to me so wide of the mark as to raise questions of criteria. Can it really be that earlier critics' high valuation of Surrey's poetry— 'worthy of a noble mind' (Sidney); 'sweet conceit' (Peacham); 'the first English classical poet' (Warton)—can their valuation have rested on a liking for such jejune crudity as the modern interpretation implies? Or can we for our part have become insensitive to forms once appreciated? And, if there has been a change in the system of preferences, is it still possible to discover, at least, the qualities in Surrey that used to be so highly valued?

Writing in 1815, that good scholar G. F. Nott remarked the lexical precision of *The soot season*: 'new *repaired* scale', for example, exactly specifies the gradual renewal of a laminated fish-scale. But as Patricia Thomson is ready to point out, the poem's 'minute' natural history is in part mediated through literature. When we read 'The swift swallow pursueth the flies small; / The busy bee her honey now she mings' we should imagine a bird of the same feather as Chaucer's 'swalwe, mortherere of the foules smale / That maken hony of floures freshe of hewe'.[1] To this instance of literary imitation, Emrys Jones adds others. Pamphilo Sasso's *Zephiro spira e col so dolce fiato*, itself a Petrarchan variation, contains items on Surrey's list. And traditional formulae from medieval English poetry ('soot season', 'summer is come'), together with alliteration, provided the means to a playfully archaizing effect. A simple catalogue seems not very much to issue from all this artfulness. Is Surrey's logic truly as rudimentary as Serafino's? Our prejudice against the catalogue form makes us initially disinclined to notice fine structure in any work that uses it. But less unfavourably disposed readers may once have been able to follow Surrey's poetic logic easily and to see that the items of his catalogue are by no means random examples of spring phenomena.

> The soot season, that bud and bloom forth brings,
> With green hath clad the hill and eke the vale:
> The nightingale with feathers new she sings:
> The turtle to her make hath told her tale:
> Summer is come, for every spray now springs,
> The hart hath hung his old head on the pale:
> The buck in brake his winter coat he flings:

---

[1] *The parliament of fowls* 353–4; Thomson 205.

The fishes fleet with new repaired scale:
The adder all her slough away she slings:
The swift swallow pursueth the flies small:
The busy bee her honey now she mings:
Winter is worn that was the flowers' bale:
   And thus I see among these pleasant things
   Each care decays, and yet my sorrow springs.
     Tottel's Miscellany (1557)

One form of arrangement is pairing. It first appears in archaizing doublets: 'bud and bloom', 'the hill and eke the vale'. And everyone must have noticed that the dove tells her tale to her mate, in implicit contrast to the speaker, who has no-one to tell his tale to—except, in the end, the reader. (The turtle-dove was a type of faithful love, or more specifically of love continuing faithful after loss.[2]) It is less obvious that all the events of spring are arranged in twos. The catalogue begins and ends with a brace of species of 'fowls', creatures that fly: nightingale, dove; swallow, bee. Between come a yoke of very closely related animals (hart, buck) and representatives of the two remaining broad kinds (fish, reptiles).[3] The kinds of life are thus reviewed with maximum variety, in such a manner as to convey indirectly a universal pairing-off.

Some of the pairs are more suggestive of temporal stages. The initial formula 'bud and bloom' sets up a type of seasonal succession to which other pairs, even though widely sundered, conform. For example 'Summer is come' finds a successor eight lines later in 'Winter is worn'. The latter phrase, however, ostensibly functions as an inverted repetition of the same statement; so that the effect is a suggestion of cyclical recurrence, sameness in difference. 'Each thing renews', as the title promises; but it does so by setting aside another old, worn, or decayed thing—'old head', 'winter coat', 'slough', 'care'. In consequence the old and the new are simultaneously present.

The most beautiful instance of the pattern is an apparent exception to it: 'The fishes fleet with new repaired scale'. The fishes are conspicuously plural not merely because 'fertile be the floods in generation' but in order to allude to Pisces, last of the winter signs. When

---

[2] See e.g. P. Valeriano *Hieroglyphica* 22.16 '*Continentissima viduitas*' (Frankfurt 1614) 267.
[3] For four-fold taxonomies of living creatures see P. Bongo *Numerorum mysteria* (Bergamo 1591) 202.

the Fishes 'fleet' (wear) and Sol enters Aries, the first summer sign, winter is indeed worn.[4] But just as Pisces is the last of the winter signs, so Libra, the 'scale', is the first—'new repaired'. Even winter is no exception to the pattern of renewal. The sonnet's most obvious structural division, its octave, begins with the soot season and ends with Libra, the autumn equinoctial sign. Simultaneously, therefore, the movement runs forward from spring to Libra 'through the six summer signs and retrospectively from Pisces to Libra through the winter signs. The cycle is complete, so that the serpent which symbolizes that cycle can aptly follow.[5]

In the same spirit the hart is said to hang up old antlers rather than to grow new ones. The bee 'mings' (remembers) the new season's task but at the same time, by implication, remembers the honey of past seasons. And the migratory swallow, whose arrival signifies spring at one level, at another conveys the fleeting yet cyclical character of time itself:[6] its swiftness is poignant to more than the flies. Thus the nature imagery shows new growth and generation as a remedy of time.

We also diminish Surrey's poem if we regard it as portraying natural renewal only, glozing over its ambivalent intimations of death. It works throughout towards the exquisitely balanced double paradox of the last line: 'Each care decays, and yet my sorrow springs'. The release of others from care is also a decay; his own sorrow is also a spring of life. But, since *decays* could be transitive, the line equally implies that care wastes him, and still his sorrow increases. Surrey claims to have seen joy and woe woven fine in the items catalogued, 'among these pleasant things'; and critics have arbitrarily disallowed that claim. But an appeal to farther thought may reverse this by showing the grounds of the conclusion in earlier alternations of old with new, life with death, positive with negative statements. They can be seen, for example, in the six-year-old hart, for whom renewal means relief of a physical irritation, but also the laying aside of the equipment of his previous breeding season as a stag. Likewise in the serpent, who may

---

[4] *OED* s.v. *Fleet* 9: 'wear, fade'. Surrey puns however with *fleet* 1, 2, 4 = float, swim; cf. *Winner and Waster* 386 'fishes flete in the flode'. *Fleet*, spelled *flete*, is the reading of every early edn except the first, which has *flote*.
[5] Tervarent col. 349 cites Martianus Capella and Servius; cf. C. Ripa *Iconolgoa* (Rome 1603) 482. Some authors connected the serpent specifically with the ecliptic: e.g. Macrobius *Saturn.* 1.9 and 19.
[6] As in Keats *To Autumn* and Dylan Thomas *Fern Hill*.

be a symbol of eternity or a fatally poisonous adder.[7] And the swallow's pursuit, which has the lethal swiftness of time itself, perhaps anticipates and catches the next line's item, to make him as much a murderer of bees as Chaucer's swallow. Here the personal application is strong: the bee, like the nightingale, readily functions as an emblem of the poet,[8] in a context where other images are similarly applied ('The nightingale . . . sings': 'The turtle . . . hath told her tale'). So it is a doomed bee-poet who remembers ('mings') honey and indeed *mixes* ('mengs')[9] it; mingling poetic sweets with the bitterness of experience, or bitterness with the sweetness of spring. No less paradoxically, the nightingale, who is also an unhappy lover, pays attention to formal innovation and sings 'with feathers new' an imitation of Petrarch. Thus the eight-line cycle of life begins and ends with emblems of the poet. The 'pleasant things' between, his experiences, have a sad resonance. They are like clothing that will be put off, until at length winter is worn in a new sense altogether.

The soot season exploits the resources of language and associative imagery so intensively, to produce so rich a yield of condensed meaning, that it is unexpectedly hard to interpret. Contrary to what one supposed, discriminating sensitivity is needed to tune even the poem's signals, let alone their overtones. It would not be ridiculous, for example, to ask how, in view of the foregoing, we should think of the hart's 'old head': is it exactly auspicious, in this context of love complaint? The same difficulty, of knowing where to stop the critical enquiry (a difficulty which hardly arises with Wyatt), confronts us in Surrey's structural patterns. These arrangements of words, things and ideas cannot be dismissed as mere decorative ornament. But to say how intentionally and publicly they are meant is far from easy.

Schemes in "Wyatt Resteth Here".

We have a good chance to study Surrey's use of an unquestionably intentional scheme in *Wyatt resteth here*. It may be natural to evoke the dead by description; but it was conventional in an encomium to

---

[7] *Adder* could still mean simply serpent (*OED* 1), though the restricted sense ('small venomous serpent', *OED* 2) was available.
[8] See R. J. Clements *Picta poesis* (Rome 1960) 184–5; also 70, 82. The underlying idea is of gathering sweetness from flowers of past literature.
[9] *Mings* was a common form of *mengs* = 'mix, mingle, blend' (*OED* s.v. *Meng* v.), so that 'mings' is a good pun.

praise by means of a blazon, a catalogue of virtues or other features.[10] Surrey's structural idea is to combine a corporal blazon with the scheme of the Seven Gifts of the Holy Ghost, correlating them so as to suggest the virtuous endowment of a whole 'manhood's shape'. In this he acknowledges a tradition that associated the Gifts with other sevenfold schemes, particularly systems of virtues (distinct from the theological and cardinal virtues); opposing vices; Beatitudes; and planetary deities. The commonest arrangement was that shown in the following table:

Table 1

Gift of the Holy Ghost	Vice	Virtue	Beatitude 'Blessed are . . .'	Planet
1 *timor domini*	*superbia*	*humilitas*	the poor in spirit	*Luna*
2 *pietas*	*invidia*	*mansuetudo*	the meek	*Mercurius*
3 *scientia*	*ira*	*temperantia*	they that mourn	*Venus*
4 *fortitudo*	*accidia*	prowess	they that hunger	*Sol*
5 *consilium*	*avaritia*	*misericordia*	the merciful	*Mars*
6 *intellectus*	*luxuria/gula*	*castitas*	the clean of heart	*Iupiter*
7 *sapientia*	*luxuria/gula*	*sobrietas*	the peacemakers	*Saturnus*

The Gifts were also associated with the seven Penitential Psalms; and we may guess that Wyatt's translation of these is alluded to not only in line 35, but in Surrey's choice of form.[11]

I

W. resteth here, that quick could never rest:
    Whose heavenly gifts increased by disdain,
And virtue sank the deeper in his breast.
    Such profit he by envy could obtain.

[10] On the blazon form see H. Smith *Elizabethan Poetry* (Cambridge, Mass. 1952) Index s.v. *Blazons*; H. Weber *La création poétique au xvi⁰ siècle en France* 2 vols (Paris 1956); and D. B. Wilson *Descriptive Poetry in France from Blason to Baroque* (Manchester 1967), with many refs. For the application to elegy, with lamentation dwelling on parts of the body in turn, cf. T. Moufet *Nobilis, or a view of the life and death of a Sidney* ed. V. B. Heltzel and H. H. Hudson (San Marino, Calif. 1940) 100ff. See also ch. 5 n. 40 below.
[11] E. Jones (ed.) *Henry Howard Earl of Surrey: Poems* (Oxford 1964) 124 notes the allusion to Wyatt's translation. For the Penitential Psalms correlated with Gifts, see R. Tuve *Allegorical Imagery* (Princeton, N.J. 1966) 92, 113. On the Gifts with their correlates see ibid. 85–102, 442 *et passim*; and R. Klibansky et al. *Saturn and Melancholy* (1964) 155–7, 163–7 and nn. K. K. Ruthven relates the amorous blazon to planetary gifts in *AUMLA* 26 (1966) 198–214.

2

A head, where wisdom mysteries did frame:
  Whose hammers beat still in that lively brain,
As on a stith: where that some work of fame
  Was daily wrought, to turn to Britain's gain.

3

A visage, stern, and mild: where both did grow,
  Vice to contemn, in virtue to rejoice:
Amid great storms, whom grace assured so,
  To live upright, and smile at fortune's choice.

4

A hand, that taught, what might be said in rhyme:
  That reft Chaucer the glory of his wit:
A mark, the which (unperfected, for time)
  Some may approach, but never none shall hit.

5

A tongue, that served in foreign realms his king:
  Whose courteous talk to virtue did inflame
Each noble heart: a worthy guide to bring
  Our English youth, by travail unto fame.

6

An eye, whose judgement none affect could blind,
  Friends to allure, and foes to reconcile:
Whose piercing look did represent a mind
  With virtue fraught, reposed, void of guile.

7

A heart, where dread was never so impressed
  To hide the thought, that might the truth advance:
In neither fortune loft, nor yet repressed,
  To swell in wealth, or yield unto mischance.

8

A valiant corpse, where force, and beauty met:
  Happy, alas, too happy, but for foes:
Lived, and ran the race, that nature set:
  Of manhood's shape, where she the mould did lose.

9

But to the heavens that simple soul is fled:
  Which left with such, as covet Christ to know,
Witness of faith, that never shall be dead:
  Sent for our health, but not received so.

Thus, for our guilt, this jewel have we lost:
The earth his bones, the heavens possess his ghost.
Tottel's Miscellany (1557)

The first Gift, in stanza 2, is explicitly 'wisdom'. Wyatt's wisdom framed mysterious matter—arts, perhaps diplomatic secrets[12]—but also, the Spirit's mysteries framed Wyatt's wisdom. The hammers of mental creation worked continually ('beat still') in his head, where the hammers of a new creation may work *still*. The next Gift is characterized by evenness and balance of antithetic epithets and clauses: 'stern and mild'; 'Vice to contemn . . . virtue to rejoice' (st. 3). It is *scientia*, which bestows the virtue of temperance or measure: evenhede, *equité*. The measurableness consisted in balancing different virtues by the plumb-line of uprightness (cf. 'to live upright') with the result of a harmony of soul commonly characterized as 'patience under suffering' (cf. 'Amid great storms . . . assured').[13] *Intellectus* or 'wit' (st. 4) taught the hand 'what might be said in rhyme'. Surprisingly as it seems at first, but aptly in view of Wyatt's role as communicator, the central item is his tongue (st. 5), the organ assigned to Mercurius god of eloquence. It corresponded to the Gift of *pietas* and the virtue of amity or benignity, here manifested in the 'courteous talk' of Wyatt's virtuous ambassadorship.[14] The conspicuous loyalty of this sovereign centre stanza ('A tongue that served in foreign realms his king') suits the secular meaning of *pietas*. But it also alludes to the *pater noster* Petition correlated with *pietas*: 'Thy kingdom come'.[15] The Gift of stanza 6 is explicitly 'judgement' (*consilium*); so that the juxtaposed 'eye' suggests the divine Eye of Judgement, as well as the seven eyes in the stone of *Zechariah*, itself considered a type of the Gifts of the Holy Ghost.[16] In stanza 7, only recognition of the Gift involved (*timor dei*, 'dread') allows us to appreciate the primary meaning—not 'Nothing scared

---

[12] *OED* s.v. *Mystery*[1] II 5 c; *Mystery*[2] 2 c.
[13] Tuve *Allegorical Imagery* 94–6. The present assignment of stanzas to Gifts corrects A. Fowler *Triumphal Forms* (Cambridge 1970) 102 n. 1.
[14] Tuve ibid. 94, 129, 139; also Klibansky 166 n. on Neckham's Gifts series. The tongue's assignement to Mercurius was commonplace: see e.g. Bongo 289.   [15] Tuve ibid. 85.
[16] On the stone, see ibid. 112; on the Eye of Judgment, E. Wind *Pagan Mysteries in the Renaissance* (1968) 222 ff., 232 ff. The visionary plumbline and stone with eyes comes in *Zech.* 3.9 and 4.10 ('they . . . shall see the plummet in the hand of Zerubbabel with those seven; they are the eyes of the Lord, which run to and fro through the whole earth').

him into covering up the truth' but 'His pious reverence was never of such a rigid stamp as to make him repress what might help truth's cause'. The vice opposed to *timor dei* was *superbia*, here alluded to in the denial that Wyatt's heart was 'loft' (proud) or given 'to swell'. And the choice of 'heart' itself refers to the appropriate Beatitude, 'Blessed are the poor in spirit (heart)'. Finally Wyatt's body manifested 'force', the remaining Gift of *fortitudo*.

If the first emphasis in approaching *Wyatt resteth here* must be on the generic indicators of the seven Gifts, the next is on the individuality of Surrey's treatment of the motif. The version of the scheme that Surrey traces in Wyatt's personality and in his roles as ambassador and poet is a much modified one. Here wisdom beats out works of fame, wit serves to teach in rhyme or overgo Chaucer. Surrey's departure from the extrinsic type even presents something of a problem, in respect of sequence. The order of Gifts, as is well known, hardly varied, so that the sequence of the poem at first seems oddly confused.[17] What can have guided Surrey's *dispositio*?

The answer does not lie in the symmetrical pattern to which I have elsewhere drawn attention: stanza 2 *manufacturing imagery* | 3 *fortune* | 5 *king* | 7 *fortune* | 8 *manufacturing imagery*. That pattern, it is quite true, might be extended, to take in the correspondence of 'heavenly' in stanza 1 with 'heavens' in 9; or 'visage' (3) with 'heart' (7), implying Wyatt's frank simplicity. But such symmetries could easily have been combined with one of the conventional sequences of the Gifts. To understand the innovation that Surrey makes we have to look farther. Unexpectedly far beneath the poem's surface, in fact. The explanation lies not in any sequence of the Gifts themselves, but in that of the associated planetary deities. Usually the deities were associated with the Gifts according to their (Ptolemaic) order of proximity to Earth: *Luna, Mercurius, Venus, Sol, Mars, Iupiter, Saturnus.* Surrey's implied order of deities, however, is *Saturnus, Venus, Iupiter, Mercurius, Mars, Luna, Sol.* That is, the order of the days of the week, over which they preside—Saturday, Friday . . . Sunday.

Surrey may have had several purposes in rearranging the Gifts. The variation would have had the attraction of poetical novelty, besides the spiritual advantage of attributing yet another human scheme to the Spirit's Gifts. More to the elegiac purpose, the reverse order of the temporal sequence may allude to the process of decay that

[17] For the order, and the few variants which correlation with other heptads gave rise to, see Tuve ibid. 92–3, 101; Klibansky 166.

destroyed the mould of 'manhood's shape. However, when the week of mortal life runs its course ('the race that nature set') it leads on to the eighth day of eternity ('to the heavens that simple soul is fled'). This is expressed by the fine formal device whereby seven stanzas on Wyatt's manhood are themselves set within the context of 'the heavens' by the framing stanzas 1 and 9: the earthly seven of his 'bones' are comprehended by the heavenly nine of his 'ghost'.[18] However, this array is itself framed yet again by the addition of a couplet coda, bringing the line total of the whole poem to 38, the number of years of Wyatt's life. (We can be fairly sure that Surrey intended this, because of the familiarity of the precedent, Petrarch's 38-line Latin panegyric on his mother, who also died aged 38.)[19] Throughout the poem runs the structural idea of alternation or interweaving of mutable with spiritual. In a series of reversals manhood's mutable shape is successively endowed with eternal gifts, realized and decayed by time, raised to the heavens, enclosed in the mortal terms of time, and commemorated in the perennial monument of a form outlasting Petrarch.

The reiterated antithesis becomes epitomized in the concluding couplet, which in consequence attains a concentrated force. Each word *sounds*, extraordinarily charged with significance. *Jewel* is the precious thing lost to men and shared between earth and heaven: it is the soul of *Malachi* 3.17 ('they shall be mine . . . in that day when I make up my jewels') lost through *guilt*; it is the 'jewel of gold' (*Numbers* 31.50) of the true offering, contrasted here with the mere gilt of those left unoblated; and it is the seven-eyed precious stone of the Spirit's Gifts (*Zechariah* 3.9). The interpretative problem becomes one of knowing how soon tact should curtail demonstration of the manifold wealth of possibilities of nuance.

---

[18] See farther Fowler *Triumphal Forms* 101–2. The eighth day of the world week symbolized everlasting bliss, on the authority of St Augustine *Epist.* 55.9.17: 'the eighth day will hold eternal blessedness: because that rest, which is eternal, is received from the eighth day, not ended by it. . . .'

[19] Fowler *Triumphal Forms* 102 n.3 lists other exemplars of the tradition. On Petrarch's poem see E. H. R. Tatham *Francesco Petrarca: The First Modern Man of Letters*, vol. 1: *Early Years and Lyric Poems* (1925) 192 n. Petrarch announces his numerology explicitly: 'versiculos tibi nunc totidem, quot praebuit annos/ Vita, damus.'

The Epitaph on Clere.

Density of texture, justness of language and unexpected structural intricacy again characterize the Epitaph on Thomas Clere. This moving poem is no doubt one of those which C.S.Lewis considered to have 'permanent, though moderate, value' (p.234). Lever, who appreciates the 'clang of steel' in its strong opening, thinks that it anticipates 'not so much the major poetry of the Elizabethans as that of the Augustans' (p.50). This notion of Surrey's poetry as neo-classical has since been developed and given substance by Emrys Jones in the fine Introduction to his edition; and many of his discriminating observations about the Virgil translation might be applied to the Epitaph: 'The reader senses a continual striving after balance, parallelism, antithesis, symmetry, and pleasurable asymmetry. . . . Such writing can be said to possess "verbal beauty" in a way foreign to Chaucer, Lydgate, and Wyatt' (p.xvii). Nevertheless, the architectural impression that Surrey's best poetry can give remains largely unaccounted for. Nor will it serve, with the Clere Epitaph, to speak of 'thin strains' or formal charms entailing 'a loss of ordinary vitality', and so excuse the critic the labour of analysis.[20] Here at least we have to do with a resonant and robust completeness of personal utterance.

Norfolk sprang thee, Lambeth holds thee dead,
    Clere of the County of Cleremont, though hight,*
    Within the womb of Ormonde's race thou bred,
    And sawest thy cousin crowned in thy sight.
Shelton for love, Surrey for Lord thou chase:
    Ay me, while life did last that league was tender:
    Tracing whose steps thou sawest Kelsall blaze,
    Laundersey burnt, and battered Bullen render:
At Muttrell gates hopeless of all recure,
    Thine Earl half dead, gave in thy hand his will:
    Which cause did thee this pining death procure,
    Ere summers four† times seven thou couldst fulfil.
    Ah Clere, if love had booted, care, or cost,
    Heaven had not won, nor Earth so timely lost.
      Camden *Remains* (1605)
      (**hight*] *high* Camden   †*four*] *seven* Camden)

---

[20] ed. Jones pp.xi, xii.

A predominant impression given by the Epitaph on Clere is of finely maintained gravity. Perhaps of formal gravity, although the formality is less the restraint of inhibition than the orderliness of contemplation. In retrospect, Clere's well-completed life seems (despite Surrey's partial denial) accomplished, firm in calm epitome. The reader may feel this in the lapidary definitiveness—'pithy, quick and sententious'[21]—thought apt for epitaphs. But what he will surely feel, indeed appreciate from his earliest readings, is the ponderous force that the poem's many names bring to bear. From the first heavy rhythms of 'Norfolk sprang thee', the names have monumental weight, alabaster luminosity. It is they that embody the fullness of Clere's life, the extent of Surrey's loss. But how they acquire so much sepulchral portentousness proves harder to say. To speak of tension between the impersonality of place-names and the intimacy of personal names, or of the tone of the closure, will not satisfy for long. The means to a powerful effect seem obscurely simple and slight. What art is it the nature of this art to conceal?

Perhaps it is an art that structures names, for their profusion in so short a poem is remarkable. A model might be adduced, the epitaph on Virgil's tomb:

Mantua me genuit, Calabri rapuere, tenet nunc
Parthenope; cecini pascua rura duces.[22]

But if Surrey's idea had been only to catch this effect, he could have done it more economically—as in *From Tuscan came*. And yet the Clere Epitaph gives no sense of being loosely constructed.

Taking the names as a point of departure, we may set out their sequence: *Norfolk* | *Lambeth* | CLERE | *Cleremont* | ORMONDE | (*cousin*) | SHELTON | SURREY | *Kelsall* | *Laundersey* | *Bullen* | *Muttrell* | (CLERE). We first think of determining the number and disposition of place names (lower case) and personal names (capitalized). But here we meet anomalies that draw attention to certain constituents. There is the conspicuously unnamed 'cousin crowned' (i.e. Anne Boleyn); there is a second occurrence of Clere in the couplet; and there is a pair of names very closely connected—'Clere of the County of Cleremont'. Nevertheless, we have unambiguous totals: 4 distinct personal names, 7 place names. The next enquiry is whether this configuration matches any other. It does, as line 12 makes plain: 'Ere summers four times seven thou couldst fulfil'. The conclusion seems

---

[21] G. Puttenham *The art of English poesy* ed. G. D. Willcock and A. Walker (Cambridge 1936) 56. [22] ed. Jones 129.

reasonable that the Epitaph has 4 personal and 7 place names because Clere died in his 28th year.

However, the twelfth line itself calls for explanation: why should the age Clere failed to attain be given so particularly like this? No doubt it was convenient to avoid the metrically awkward 'twenty-eight'. But the emphatic repetition of the factors 4 and 7 points to a less trivial reason. In number symbolism, the tetrad and the heptad carried well-established, clearly defined meanings, which function in the present context with considerable aptness.

Seven was universally known as the number of mutability; of the temporal sublunary world, as opposed to the eternal; and also (contradictorily) of the eternal sabbath. It was

> The number of the unfixed fires of heaven;
> And of the eternal sacred Sabbaoth.[23]

It was therefore very suitable for elegiac forms. Moreover, it had a strong association with the body, which turned out to have 7 internal members, 7 tissues, 7 visible parts, 7 orifices, 7 directions of movement, and the like.[24] No less familiarly, 4 was the number of Friendship, League, Alliance and Concord.[25] In fact, this meaning was so fundamental as to underlie the numeration of the elements and the seasons. Whether those meanings correlate with the poem's constituents must be our next enquiry.

In the case of the tetrad of concord, it soon appears that various social relations occur not merely as topics ('Ay me . . . that league was tender') but as the basis of formal organization of the epitaph, considered as a sonnet. John Fuller analyses its division as follows:

> Clere's good connexions (related to Anne Boleyn) are presented in the first quatrain. His purely voluntary relationships ('chase' = 'chose') follow, in the second quatrain; and, arising from his association with Surrey, his selfless attention to the wounded Earl at the siege of Montreuil, leading to his death, occupies the third quatrain. There is logical development here: by contrast between the first and second quatrains and by example between the second and third. The points thus made are that whatever

[23] Du Bartas *Divine weeks* tr. J. Sylvester (1613) 361. See Fowler *Spenser and the Numbers of Time* (1964) 45–6, 248 n.; also V. F. Hopper in *PMLA* 55 (1940) 962 ff.
[24] Macrobius *In somn. Scip.* 1.6.77–82; see farther Fowler *Numbers of Time* 272.
[25] ibid. 24–6; I. C. Butler *Number Symbolism* (1970) 123. The idea goes back to Plato *Timaeus* 32.

the status of one's birth one does not choose it, and that love and friendship are on the other hand a matter of choice, thought not of calculation.[26]

To this we need only add that each quatrain of the octet presents two kinds of 'league'. In the second, it is Clere's love for Mary Shelton and his friendship or squirely relation with Surrey himself: 'Shelton for love, Surrey for Lord thou chase'. In the first, two distinct family connections are traced. 'Clere of the County of Cleremont' honours the name that Thomas Clere received from his father—the male, dynastic relation. But 'Within the womb of Ormonde's race' insists on the maternal matrix of this Cleremont seed, and hence on the Howard connection that the poem amplifies. Padelford paraphrases: 'Though of another house, the Howards claim you: you were born in Norfolk, your remains rest in our chapel, you had the blood of the Ormondes, a house united to ours by marriage'.[27] In other words, the 4 personal names imply 4 kinds of alliance, which is also the significance of the tetrad as a number symbol.

The place names represent in part the extent of Surrey's bond with Clere. Norfolk was the home of the Howards: the poet's father was Duke of Norfolk. And the last 4 place names allude to campaigns that Surrey and Clere shared. It was at the siege of Montreuil in September 1544, while caring for Surrey, that Clere received the wound from which he eventually ('pining') died, in the April of the following year. However, these are not the only ideas governing the choice of names.

The first two define the limits of Clere's bodily existence: Norfolk 'sprang' him; his corpse lies in Lambeth. Within these limits he lived the life whose relations and deeds the poem reviews. The next place name, Cleremont, comes in a phrase that unites place and person, material and spiritual aspects: 'Clere of the County of Cleremont'. As such it constitutes as it were a monad combining even and odd, material and spiritual—in contrast with the bodily dyad before it. The formulation 'County of Cleremont' also introduces the genealogical heritage on which English territorial claims in France were based. A more obvious representative value attaches to towns successfully besieged by the English: Kelsall in Scotland, Landrecy in the Netherlands, Montreuil and Boulogne debatably in France. Thus the place names divide into 3 concerned with family connections and 4

[26] *The Sonnet* (1972) 16.
[27] *The Poems of Henry Howard Earl of Surrey* ed. F. M. Padelford (Seattle, Wash. 1928) 228. Padelford's genealogy should be treated with caution.

with campaigns; perhaps hinting at the common division of the heptad as a creative 3 + 4 ('The critical and double-sexed seven . . . which three and four containeth jointly both').[28] Specification of the number of 'summers', campaigning *seasons*, again introduces the tetrad. Thus 7 is not permitted the simple value of mutability which it often has in elegies. It is strongly offset by the tetrad of alliance, which in this solemn context may be taken to imply the Pythagorean quaternion of the soul, rather than merely the body's elements or complexions.[29]

Besides these meanings, the numerical structure presents a further symbolism. Twenty-eight as the product of 'four times seven' has a precise significance in the present context. It is a perfect number, that is, one that equals the sum of its divisors ($1 + 2 + 4 + 7 + 14 = 28$). Because it neither exceeded its divisors nor fell short, a perfect number signified virtue: symbolically a desirable total for the years of a life. Now, perfect numbers were regarded as generated from terms of the even number series, arranged in pairs: 4, 8 | 16, 32 | 64, 128 | . . . . As a sixteenth-century arithmologist puts it, 'each term has a fellow' ('vides quemlibet terminum habere socium'),[30] from which one is subtracted. The resultant pairs, multiplied, form the series of perfect numbers: $4 \times 7 = 28$; $16 \times 31 = 496$; $64 \times 127 = 8128$. . . . Hence Surrey's formation of 28 from its two factors 4 and 7 specifies its function as a perfect number. While intentional, however, this meaning is nevertheless ambiguous. If we take *timely lost* = 'soon lost',[31] then the idea must be that Clere's death prevented him from making his life perfect. But if we take *timely* = 'seasonably, aptly,[32] then Clere may be thought of as achieving the perfection of virtue by the manner of his dying. In Biblical exegesis 28 denoted the dimensions of the Temple,[33] so that the completion of the spirit's dwelling would be meant—a point that adds force to Surrey's

---

[28] Du Bartas loc. cit. n.23 above; probably based on Macrobius *In somn. Scip.* 1.6.22–44 (ed. W.H.Stahl (New York and London 1966) 104–8), where 7 is a module of creation because of the structural value of its addends, esp. 3 and 4.

[29] For the distinction, see Bongo 248. But Macrobius relates elemental concord to the Pythagorean *tetraktus*, at *In somn. Scip.* 1.6.41. On Milton's use of a not dissimilar structural pattern of 4 and 7 see A.Fowler in *Silent Poetry* (1970) 178.

[30] Bongo 478; cf. Augustine *Civ. Dei* 11.30, and see M.Gardner *Sci. Amer.* 218 (Mar. 1968) 121.   [31] *OED* s.v. *Timely* adv. 1.   [32] ibid. 2.

[33] *Exo.* 26 and 36. See Bongo 473.

mention of a chapel as Clere's final place. Thus the Epitaph designed to embellish a building has itself an architectural proportion. As befits epigraphy, its significance partly lies in the arrangement of its visible words.

The formal sequence of the names may also have communicative value. Allowing for the special composite character of 'Clere of . . . Cleremont', the arrangement of place names (p) and surnames (s) is as follows: $p\,p \mid s\text{-}p \mid s\,s\,s \mid p\,p\,p\,p \mid s$. This could be seen as a form of the *tetraktus*, the Pythagorean creative principle whose terms 1, 2, 3, 4 add to 10 and so return to the divine unity. The monad, giving rise as it does to both even (material) and odd (spiritual) number-series, was regarded as simultaneously even and odd. In the same way the Clere-of-Cleremont term unites Surrey's odd (surname) series and even (place-name) series. That the *tetraktus* was called the fountain of number and virtue possibly throws light on 'Norfolk *sprang* thee'. And the return of the *tetraktus* to unity in 10 finds echo in the repetition of *Clere* in the closure. Clere's virtue elevates him into a spiritual existence transcending spatial limits. However, the significance of the *tetraktus* as *vinculum* or bond of matter and spirit persists in the final couplet, in the implication of competing bonds, heaven and earth each desiring the beloved Clere.

We have still to account for the anomaly noted earlier, the un-named 'cousin'. Anne Boleyn had been executed after three years as Henry 8's consort, so that it might be thought tactless of Surrey, even writing four consorts later, to spell out the dangerous name. But then, it might be tactless to introduce Anne at all, if his purpose was to display Clere's good connections. One explanation is that Surrey's own connection with Clere was through the Boleyns (see table 2). The argument of the Epitaph, which amplifies the bonds between Clere and the Howards, thus called for some mention of the Boleyns. But Surrey goes farther. He silently reaffirms the rank of Anne Boleyn, by according her a formal position of dignity. The 'cousin crowned' comes in the central position of sovereignty among the people mentioned: *Clere | Ormond | (cousin) | Shelton | Surrey*. This array does not conflict with any of the pattern traced earlier, since Anne is not actually named (except for the punning hint in 'Bullen').

I have deliberately pushed this interpretation farther than wisdom would have determined for a purely critical study. But the present aim is only to sketch loosely something of the range of possibilities for indirect meaning in Surrey's poetry. The difficulty it presents is not

Table 2

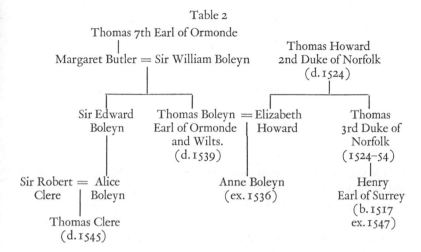

usually that of finding the primary meaning: we may well think the meaning of a poem such as the Clere epitaph lucid beyond dispute. The difficulty is rather to know how much nuance and structural reinforcement Surrey intended. Some formal structure must indubitably be intentional and 'part of the poem' in every imaginable reconstruction that we should call valid. But with the possibility of so much, doubts arise on several counts: the probability of an intention so complex; the possibility of excluding the critic's insidious creativity; the desirability, even, of completely intentional order. These problems are not necessarily accompaniments of high poetic value. But they are its common accompaniments. And their presence goes some way towards explaining why Surrey's poetry seemed so important to his successors. More than Wyatt's it offered models of indirection, of formal richness, of subtle recourses of form, of distinctively poetic inexhaustibility.

3

Sestina Structure in
Ye Goatherd Gods

═══════

Of Elizabethan poems that resist the approaches of modern criticism
Sidney's double sestina *Ye goatherd gods* is a notable, indeed a noble,
example. Its diction and syntax are a little too simple for explanation;
its direct statements appear to contain nothing difficult; and its
imagery can easily be passed over as 'so shopworn that to admire the
poem almost seems a literary affectation.'[1] Yet it continues to give
an unusual impression of force, as if it were creative, and it continues to resist many a resolute effort at interpretation, as if it
were complex. William Empson's historically important analysis, in
Seven Types of Ambiguity, directs attention to the various 'ambiguities'
that the sestina's end words are made to bear (or can be brought to
bear): 'the form takes its effect by concentrating on these words and
slowly building up our interest in them; all their latent implications
are brought out by the repetitions.' The result is that 'when the sta-
tic conception of the complaint has been finally brought into light
. . . a whole succession of feelings about the local scenery . . . has
been enlisted into sorrow and beats as a single passion of the mind.'[2]
However, Empson's roster of usages did little to illuminate their
order and significance, far less the overwhelming superiority of
Sidney's composition to, say, Sannazaro's *Chi vuole udire i miei sospiri in
rime*.[3] David Kalstone, similarly, although he has profited from
Empson's hint about 'the sustained magnificence of its crescendo'
and given the best account of the sestina's emotional progression,
commits himself to few propositions about its meaning.[4] He shows
Sidney's landscape to be endowed with more symbolic values than
Sannazaro's, without saying much about what these values are. It is

[1] J. C. Ransom *The New Criticism* (Norfolk, Conn. 1941) 108–14.
[2] *Seven Types of Ambiguity* (1947) 38.
[3] J. Sannazaro *Arcadia* 4; *Opere volgari* ed. A. Mauro (Bari 1961) 29–31.
[4] *Sidney's Poetry: Contexts and Interpretations* (Cambridge, Mass. 1965).

not just a matter of his happening to dwell on one model (Sannazaro) rather than another (Montemayor), or of underestimating the extent of Sidney's return to Petrarch's own transformation of the pastoral world into symbols of inner experience. Instead the confusion is a general one: the difficulty we all feel in face of the best mannerist lyrics. The poetry invites yet baffles criticism.

This has at least two causes. First, as with modernist poetry—and it is Wallace Stevens's that comes to mind as a twentieth-century analogue to Sidney's—many of the effects of mannerism are sophisticated finesses on earlier poetic conventions. Where we cannot recognize generic types, we are bound to find individual departures from them puzzling. Thus, no critic is likely to get very far with *Ye goatherd gods* until he recognizes the generic innovation whereby the singing-contest variation of pastoral eclogue is combined with the sestina love-complaint, as in Sannazaro, and then farther transformed by abstraction into an interiorized philosophical ode. This tertiary form has its own highly economical signal system, not all of which we may hope to recover. But at least we can make a start with such broad features as difference in stance between participants in a singing contest.[5] The second cause of difficulty is that much of the rhetorical and metrical repertoire of the sixteenth century has become unfamiliar. A formidable obstacle, this, since much of a mannerist poem may be conveyed through just such formal channels of communication. In the case of the sestina form knowledge of the interpretative implications has disappeared so completely that this must be our point of departure.

Sestina Form.

Sestinas normally consist of six unrhymed six-line stanzas with a tercet *congedo* or envoy. What characterizes this exacting form is a repetition of the same endwords in each stanza, in positions continually varied according to a strict rule. In the *congedo*, all 6 repeated words occur, 3 in medial and 3 in terminal positions. Even ignoring *congedo* variations, there are a great many possible plans—in fact, 719 —by which a sestina's endwords might in principle be permuted. However, almost all real sestinas obey one particular rule, whereby

---

[5] See below, 'Strephon and Klaius'. For differentiation in another singing contest, between Lalus and Dorus, see N.L. Rudenstine *Sidney's Poetic Development* (Cambridge, Mass. 1967) 82 ff.

the endwords 1 2 3 4 5 6 of any stanza are reordered to form the sequence 6 1 5 2 4 3 in the next. The only existing explanation of the rule is genetic: namely, that Arnaut Daniel takes his departure from from the simpler transformation rule of a Peire de Cazals poem (6 5 4 3 2 1) and 'instead of repeating the rhyme-words of the first strophe from the bottom up . . . takes them alternately from bottom up and top down'.[6] But this fails to account for the particular departure that Arnaut Daniel chose to make. A partial answer may lie in the fact that the rule forms pairs of digits each with 7 as their sum: 6 + 1 | 5 + 2 | 4 + 3. The early sestina was used for sombre love complaints to which the elegiac 7 had obvious aptness.[7]

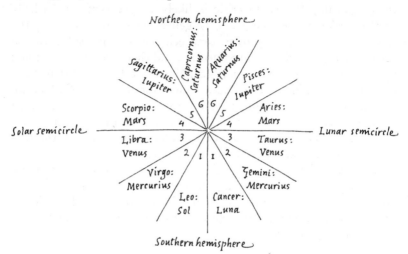

But an adequate account of the sestina form would also have to explain its relation to a similar pattern in the zodiac, to which the astronomical content of the first Italian sestina, Dante's authoritative *Al poco giorno ed al gran cerchio d'ombra*, directs our attention. A normal sestina's endword sequence matches the sequence of corresponding solar and lunar zodiacal signs. The Ptolemaic division of signs between the chief luminaries followed a regular order whereby the pair closest to the zenith, Leo and Cancer, were assigned to Sol and Luna themselves; the next pair, Gemini and Virgo, to the most proximate

---

[6] F.J.A.Davidson in *MLN* 25 (1910) 18–20; cf. A.Jeanroy in *Romania* 42 (1912), and J. Roubaud 'La sextine d'Arnaut Daniel' *Change* 2 (1969).
[7] On 7 as an elegiac number see above 33 n. 23.

planet, Mercury; Taurus and Libra to the next nearest, Venus; and so on round the zodiac (see fig. opposite).[8]

This distribution from alternate sides, particularly if we consider signs of the northern hemisphere alone (*Scorpio | Aries | Sagittarius | Pisces | Capricornus | Aquarius*), very much resembles the distribution of repeated words from alternate ends of a sestina stanza, working in to the middle. Moreover, pairs of numbers designating opposed signs add to 7, and make the familiar sequence 6 1 5 2 4 3 , starting from the solstitial point. Thus Dante's ode, which explicitly mentions the winter solstice ('Al poco giorno'), and which like many sestinas after it dwells on imagery of light and dark,[9] may be meant to render in its stanzaic structure the sun's annual course round the ecliptic. In that movement, the compensated equipoise of opposed signs at semi-annual intervals, or of corresponding nocturnal and diurnal hours, offers a marvel of order that has inspired more than one poetic meditation.[10] Of course the sestina rule was no doubt followed slavishly by many who regarded it as a purely abstract convention. Even so, the underlying principle seems often to have been applied in one respect: namely, that close attention was given to the pairing of endwords. In Dante's seminal ode, indeed, the pairs (*ombra–colli, erba–verde, pietra–donna*) are linked syntactically: 'pietra . . . sente come fosse donna'.[11]

Occasionally, however, the endwords form threes. This grouping may have a similar origin, in an alternative analysis of the sestina cycle. If we analyse the cycle *ordinally*, the first endword of any stanza becomes the second in the next, the second endword becomes the fourth . . . and the sixth becomes the first; so that the ordinal formula is 2 4 6 5 3 1. Expressed as a rule 'Taken even-number endwords in ascending order, odd-number endwords in descending order', it might lead to the division 3 + 3. It is worth noting that the sestina

---

[8] See Ptolemy *Tetrabiblos* 1.17; ed. F.E.Robbins (1940) 79–81.
[9] As the endwords reflect. In Petrarch's *Canzoniere* alone, no. 332 has *lieto, notti*; 142 *lume, cielo*; 22 *sole, giorno, alba*; 237 *luna, notte, sera*. Pontus de Tyard's *Lors que Phebus sue le long du jour*, probably the first French sestina, abounds in temporal and astronomical imagery.
[10] Spenser's is discussed in A.K.Hieatt *Short Time's Endless Monument* (New York 1960) 39–40 *et passim*.
[11] Canzone 1.5–6. Cf. Petrarch *Canzoniere* 142, with almost equally obvious pairing (*frondi–rami, lume–tempo, cielo–poggi*); *Canzoniere* 22 (*sole–stelle, alba–giorno, terra–selva*); and Pontus de Tyard *Oeuvres poétiques complètes* ed. J.C.Lapp (Paris 1966) 97–9 (*jour–nuits*).

envoy uses both groupings. Whichever variant order it follows, it introduces the repeated words in pairs (2 per line) and in threes (3 medially, 3 terminally).[12]

Such sestinas as Petrarch's *Non ha tanti animali il mar fra l'onde* (*Canz.* 237) explore the thematic possibilities of grouped endwords with some subtlety. An obvious literal pairing *onde—luna, sera—notte, boschi—piaggia* counterpoints with a division into the terrestrial landscape features *onde—boschi—piaggia* and the astronomical entities *luna—notte—sera*. The sustained meditation on endwords interrelated in this way naturally evolves interiorising symbolisms: *sera* means the evening of the lover's death; *onde* the tears that flow from the living earth ('vivo terren') of his body; and *boschi* his passionate isolation from society— 'Amor femmi un cittadin de' boschi'; 'Love has made me a free-burgess of the forest'.[13] Sidney could thus find in the Petrarchan tradition a rich store of models for the symbolic development of sestina endwords; and could even perhaps assume familiarity with the idea of grouping them in alternative ways.

His own endwords form highly significant arrays. The initial sequence gives the literally antithetic pairs *mountains—vallies* and *morning—evening*, thus leading us to see a less explicit antithesis in the remaining pair *forests* (nature, wildness, passion, material ὕλη) and *music* (art, immaterial harmony, civilization). The more obvious pairs imply extremes of experience. Both transform familiar consolatory proverbs—Every mountain has its valley; Every day the night comes; After night comes the day[14]—into their opposites. But Sidney's mountains and vallies are also situated in the Petrarchan *paysage moralisé*: Klaius' distaste at 'the flowers of these vallies' recalls 'a me non val fiorir di valli' and Strephon's 'dark vallies' the 'ombrose valli' sought by beasts in another sestina complaint.[15] And we may

---

[12] The commonest order was 2, 5 | 4, 3 | 6, 1; but Sidney adopts the Petrarchan variant 1, 2 | 3, 4 | 5, 6 used for *Canzoniere* 332. The French envoy in 4 lines is no exception; it pairs repeated words 1, 2 | 4, 5 | 3 | 6.

[13] cf. also *Canzoniere* 66, where literal pairs *nebbia – venti, pioggia – ghiaccio, fiumi – valli* counterpoint with a (3 + 3) terrestrial–aerial division, and interiorizing is prominent (winds called *amorosi* or *dolorosi* provoke clouds of disapproval or disdain). Pontus de Tyard's *Lors que Phebus* is more complex still: besides contrasting pairs (*jour–nuits, sejour–eternelle*) and threes (temporal–atemporal) it has a system of *rhyming* pairs.

[14] These also occur together in Pandarus' advice to Troilus, *Troilus and Criseyde* 1.950–2, following Alan of Lille *Liber parabolarum*, Migne *P.L.* 210.582. See also Tilley D 59, 70, H 467, N 164. [15] Petrarch *Canzoniere* 66.19 and 26.

also glimpse a vista of the landscape which lies behind all of these, that of the *Anticlaudianus*, with its 'vallis abyssus' and 'celsi praeceps audacia montis', the difficulties Prudentia must pass to reach God.[16]

Scarcely less obvious than the antithetic pairing of endwords is the grouping in threes. *Mountains, vallies* and *forests* are all features of the natural landscape; whereas *morning, evening* and *music* all imply temporal measure.

Since the envoy lines, like the stanzas, are shared between Strephon and Klaius, the endwords themselves, on their final occurrence, fall to one or other singer: a fact that may be not without significance. The folio editions differ from the *Old Arcadia* and the 1590 *Arcadia* in assigning the second-last line to Strephon. However, all agree that the 'natural' pair *mountains–vallies* is Strephon's, the temporal pair *morning–evening* Klaius'.

Strephon and Klaius.

Elaborate formal resemblances between Strephon's and Klaius' stanzas constitute a striking feature of the ode. Since the two lovers' attitudes are brought into such direct and frequent comparison, a subject of early enquiry ought to be how far they agree or differ. We find that *Ye goatherd gods* itself, the 1590 *Arcadia* I.I, and the unfinished *Lamon's Tale*[17] included in the 1593 *Arcadia* all concur in differentiating 'the hopeless shepherd Strephon' and 'the pastor Klaius' clearly.[18] The differences fit their ages. For example Klaius 'the other in some years did pass/ And in those gifts that years distribute': he is generally 'wise Klaius'.[19] But the polarity is too fully imagined to be resolved into a schematic antithesis. Thus Klaius, although for 'shepherd's art/ Among the wisest . . . accounted wise', was 'Yet not so wise as of unstained heart'; and although 'Strephon was young' he learnt so humbly from his elders 'that the grave did not his words despise'.[20] When they first love Urania, Strephon leaps with 'joy and jollity' whereas Klaius fights the fever of passion and only follows her 'in spite of wisdom's song'; but when they lose her it is Strephon who

[16] Alan of Lille *Anticlaudianus* 2.3; Migne *P.L.* 210.500 (tr. W.H. Cornog (Philadelphia, Pa 1935) 67), a passage imitated elsewhere in *Ye goatherd gods*. However, moralized contrasts of hill and valley were commonplace: e.g. Drayton *Polyolbion* 7.62–92, 14.81.
[17] Ptd in 1593 *Arcadia* with the 1st Eclogues; Other Poems 4 in *The Poems of Sir Philip Sidney* ed. W. A. Ringler (Oxford 1962) 242–56.
[18] 1590 *Arcadia* I.I; ed. A. Feuillerat (Cambridge 1965) 5.
[19] *Lamon's Tale* 21–2 (cf. 24, 36) and 419.   [20] ibid. 33–8.

weeps in 'languishing remembrance', Klaius who exhorts to 'joy in the midst of all woes'.[21] The subtlety of the half-contrasting, half-complementary relation anticipates that of *L'Allegro* and *Il Penseroso*.

By far the most perceptive account of Strephon and Klaius is A. C. Hamilton's. He sees that Strephon's mere lament at the loss of Urania is answered by Klaius, who dwells rather on the positive gain from their experience. Klaius exhorts Strephon to 'think with consideration' about Urania's virtue as well as her beauty: 'He catalogues what they have gained through loving her: they have moved (in ascending order) from knowledge more than ordinary, to heavenly knowledge, and then to knowledge of themselves.'[22]

This suggestion of a Platonic *askesis* seems entirely justified. Klaius certainly aspires beyond beauty: 'as the greatest thing the world can show, is her beauty, so the least thing that may be praised in her, is her beauty.' He speaks of the experience of love as raising their thoughts 'above the ordinary level of the world, so as great clerks do not disdain [their] conference';[23] as leading them to cosmic contemplation while others sleep. And his claim that Urania has 'given eyes unto Cupid' seems even to introduce the notion of divine love. Nor does Strephon quite contradict this, for he speaks of 'reverence and desire' dividing Klaius. If Sidney means the sort of Platonic love that can 'raise up our thoughts' by progressive stages, we are tempted to think of Strephon and Klaius as representing two of these stages.[24] This notion is particularly attractive, since it accommodates the similarities as well as the differences between Strephon and Klaius. Indeed, it would almost imply identity. The two would be sub-characters generated from the same lover, or successive cross-sections of a super-character's time-worm.[25] In several passages *Lamon's Tale* could be taken to imply some such interiorization. Not only are we told that 'Klaius' soul did in his Strephon rest' (l. 29) but that 'He found man's virtue is but part of man,/ And part must follow where whole man doth go' (421-2).

Sidney has developed the distinction between Strephon and Klaius most delicately in *Ye goatherd gods*, where a complex system of paired

[21] ibid. 170-7, 222; 1590 *Arcadia* I.I; ed. Feuillerat 6–7.

[22] A. C. Hamilton 'Sidney's *Arcadia* as Prose Fiction: Its Relation to Its Sources' *ELR* 2 (1972) 49–50.

[23] 1590 *Arcadia* I.I; ed. Feuillerat 7.   [24] ibid. 8, 6, 7.

[25] For the generation of allegorical subcharacters see A. Fletcher *Allegory: The Theory of a Symbolic Mode* (Ithaca, N.Y. 1958) 25–69, 195 *et passim*.

constituents allows him to draw the finest of contrasts with economy. Every commentator has noticed that each pair of stanzas forms a unit, a twelve-line microcosm of the twelve-stanza ode, consisting of a statement by Strephon and Klaius' answer. David Kalstone, who treats the lovers as almost indistinguishable,[26] observes farther that the ceremonious opening invocations correspond; that with one exception each pair of stanzas 'maintains a rigid grammatical parallelism'; and that at stanzas 9 and 10 the climax of the poems' emotional crescendo exceptionally breaks the form—'Strephon's speech displays more violence' whereas Klaius sees the reflexiveness of violence and recognizes 'his isolation from the ceremonies of the poem':[27] 'And stop mine ears, lest I grow mad with music'. Against the music that maddens the music of Urania, 'whose parts maintained a perfect music', is immediately counterpoised. And the last pair of stanzas resumes the pattern of anaphora and parison, though its 'recollected harmony' does not relieve the poems' despair. (The last stanzas' division—emphasized by syntactical suspension—into 4 lines of recollection and 2 of lament has, however, the 2:1 proportion of the diapason, which recovers one harmony.) To all this it may be added that the parallelism, if 'rigid', is nevertheless very varied, ranging as it does from a repeated whole line (ll. 4, 11), through anaphora and parison in differing positions,[28] assonantal echo,[29] lexical and syntactic echo,[30] to structural resemblance.[31] Other parallels are more elastic than rigid. The anaphoras at lines 28-9 and 34-5 are transposed, as are the noun–verb continuations of those at lines 13, 15 and 19, 21 ('I that was once free-burgess . . . I that was once esteemed' and 'I that was once delighted . . . I that was once the music'); and Klaius' stanza 8 repeats Strephon's progression *see–hear–feel* in a permuted form.

[26] e.g. 78: 'the lovers' former state as free hunters and musicians'. Sidney's Strephon is not a hunter.
[27] ibid. 79, 81. According to Kalstone, Sidney 'breaks the rigid parallelism' at sts 9–10. But the stanzas only modulate the pattern: their first halves correspond by *anaphora* and *adnominatio* (Klaius replacing Strephon's nominative 'I' with oblique cases), there are other anaphoric links ('I wish', 'and', 'curse' and 'hate'), and throughout they maintain close semantic resemblance.
[28] Lines 1, 3 in sts 3–4 ('I that was once'); ll. 1, 4, 5 in sts 5–6 ('Long since'); ll. 1, 3, 5 in sts 7–8 ('Me seems I'); l. 1 in sts 11–12 ('For she').
[29] e.g. l. 2 in sts 5–6.
[30] e.g. sts 1–2, pronoun number; sts 9–10, pronoun case; sts 11–12, relative clauses, delay of verb.
[31] e.g. *dispositio* of stanza parts, as with the invocations of sts 1–2.

Moreover, there are additional correspondences, outside the main system, between contiguous but non-pairing stanzas.[32] Again, extra, medial occurrences of the endword *evening* in stanzas 9 and 10 prompt us to look for similar extra occurrences in the corresponding stanza pair in the sestina's first cycle—where we find one in Klaius' stanza (*music*, l. 21) but not in Strephon's. It would be impracticable and tedious to complete the catalogue. But the system of correspondences may already be thought intricate enough to justify unusually close comparison of the singers' parts, which like Urania's maintain a music, even if hardly one in unison.

Prominent in the first pair of stanzas is Klaius' transformation of Strephon's 'grassy mountains', 'pleasant vallies' and 'quiet forests' to 'savage', 'woeful' and 'secret'. This darker view reflects Klaius' melancholy as well as his rivalry of Strephon's complaint. But it also expresses his usual attitude to nature. He has little empathy with forests, the wild contrary of civilized order. Strephon can describe himself in Petrarchan diction as 'free-burgess of the forests' (l. 13), but that would be unthinkable for Klaius, who actually took delight in 'hunting the wild inhabiters of forests'. The hunt should be understood allegorically, as the moral persecution of desire.[33] Initially desire was the quarry of Klaius' moral reason; and when he himself succumbs in turn, he can say with nice ambiguity 'my thoughts chase me like beasts in forests' (l. 35). His 'failure' by no means neutralizes the polarity between Strephon's association with what is natural, wild, or passionate, and Klaius' with what is civilized, orderly, or rational. As their affective Fall continues, Strephon's despair banishes him from the amorous forest, whereas Klaius is more dreadfully involved in it. Strephon's thoughts become 'more desert . . . than forests', that is, wilder than nature. Klaius', however, become natural; they are beasts that chase him, perhaps like Actaeon's dogs, which were commonly given a psychological interpretation: 'Actaeon, neglecting the pursuit of virtue and heroical actions, puts off the mind of a man, and degenerates into a beast'.[34]

---

[32] e.g. *sun* mentioned in similar places in sts 8–9.

[33] On the symbolic hunt see E. Panofsky *Renaissance and Renascences in Western Art* (1970) 91 n. Petrarch's 'Amor femmi un cittadin de' boschi' (*Canzoniere* 237) expressed an idea still familiar to Dryden, whose love-melancholic Anthony fancies himself 'turned wild': 'The herd', he says 'take me for their fellow-citizen' (*All for love* 1.232, 241–3).

[34] G. Sandys *Ovid's metamorphosis Englished, mythologized* (1632) 100. It was commoner still, however, to apply the myth against presumption in judging

The second, and darker, half of the sestina laments more objective changes. These affect both the 'spoiled forests' (l. 71) of nature and the music of social harmony. Now Strephon curses the very inventors of music (l. 51), while Klaius, shamed by his error into self-hatred,[35] fears to be driven mad by the demands of order (for which the demanding sestina form has become an exquisitely apt symbol), and finds music replaced, in his guilty ears, by 'dreadful cries of murdered men' (l. 48). To understand this mysterious passage we have to recall that Klaius himself 'was once the music' (order) of the vallies: a music later replaced by unharmonious 'cries in stead of music' (ll. 21, 24). By contrast, Strephon is associated only at a remove with natural order (music), in the form of bird song (the nightingale's, owl's, or 'deadly swannish music': ll. 40, 18, 25). The deterioration in bird song—'the nightingales do learn of owls their music'—alludes to Theocritus' First Idyll, which develops the theme of the upside-down world: 'Daphnis is dying: now let the deer worry dogs/ And from the mountains let owls to the nightingales sing'.[36] However, Sidney's specification of 'screech-owl' (l. 18), in a context of ruined order and cries of the dead, recalls the very different treatment of a similar motif, *Isaiah* 34. In this great vision of divine vengeance, which provided Milton with images of desolation for his fallen world,[37] comes the difficult verse 'There shall meet also Ziim and Iim, and the satyr shall cry to his fellow, and the screech owl shall rest there' (34.14, Geneva), 'Et occurrent daemonia onocentauris, et pilosus clamabit alter ad alterum; ibi cubavit lamia' (Vulgate). Abraham Cowley, who imitates the verse in 'Th'unburied ghosts shall sadly moan,/ The satyrs laugh to hear them groan',[38] comments: 'The English mentions only

[35] Line 59, 'Shamed I hate my self in sight of mountains', perhaps with a precise allegory: cf. Sir J. Harington *Ludovico Ariosto's 'Orlando Furioso' Translated into English Heroical Verse* ed. R. McNulty (Oxford 1972) 80 'the mountain which in the scripture it self is taken for preachers, as St Augustine noteth'—an idea doubtless taken from S. Fornari *La spositione sopra 'L' Orlando Furioso'* (Florence 1549–50) 4.49–50.
[36] Δάφνις ἐπεὶ θνάσκει, καὶ τὰς κύνας ὤλαφος ἕλκοι,/ κἠξ ὀρέων τοι σκῶπες ἀηδόσι γαρύσαιντο; discussed in Otis 116.
[37] e.g. *Is.*34.11, echoed in the gull-haunted island of *Par. Lost* 11.835.
[38] A. Cowley *Poems* ed. A. R. Waller (Cambridge 1905) 214; cf. *Lamon's Tale* 507, where Strephon hears 'of ghosts . . . the ghastly cries'.

the affairs of great men or gods: see D. T. Starnes and E. W. Talbert *Classical Myth and Legend in Renaissance Dictionaries* (Chapel Hill, N.C. 1955) 206–7, 436–7. Is it coincidence that Actaeon had a dog called Urania (Hyginus *Fab.* 181 'Diana')?

satyrs, the Latin besides that (for *pilosi* are the same) *daemonia*, and *lamiae*, *hobgoblings*. The Hebrew is said to signify *nocturnum spectrum*, an appearance of something in the night. From whence the Chaldees [*sc.* Aramaeans] translate it, an *owl*, the English a screech-owl.'[39] It might be wrong to infer from this context that the 'noisome scent' and 'cries of murdered men' of Sidney's poem come from those slaughtered in the *dies irae*.[40] But I think we are obliged to see the desolation of Urania's departure as a vision of cosmic implication: the Biblical allusion would have been inappropriate if the meaning had been only erotic. One begins to think that Klaius' fire 'is more, than can be made with forests' because it is spiritual, like the fire of judgement in *Isaiah* 30 or 33.

The final pair of stanzas contrast Strephon's self-absorption ('Hath cast *me*, wretch, into eternal evening') with Klaius' social concern ('*our* spoiled forests . . . *our* best pastured mountains'). 'Eternal evening' counts against Strephon if it is dramatizing exaggeration, and even more if it is not. But his destructive violence in stanza 9 and his rival's drawing back from madness in stanza 10 may mean that Strephon is the more afflicted mentally.[41] As Robert Burton remarks, if a lover's melancholy 'be violent, or his disease inveterate . . . both imagination and reason are misaffected, first one and then the other'.[42]

The Invocations.

At the level of seriousness argued for above, it cannot be a matter of indifference what powers Strephon and Klaius invoke. Besides, the repetition of a whole line in stanzas 1 and 2 (no doubt to draw attention by its shifting position to the formal principle of the sestina) implies the closest equivalence between their contents, and especially

[39] Cowley ed. Waller 219. The owl was commonly of ill omen, as at *Aen.* 4.462 to guilty Dido. But Sidney may have been influenced by an etymological connection of *ulula* (screech-owl) with *elegy*: see J. C. Scaliger *Poetice* 1.50 (Lyons 1561) 52C. Surprisingly, 'Swannish music' had also a moral: it shows up corruption in *Old Arcadia* Poem 10.73–87.

[40] *Is.* 34.2–3 (Geneva): 'the indignation of the Lord is upon all nations . . . he hath . . . delivered them to the slaughter. And their slain shall be cast out, and their stink shall come up out of their bodies, and the mountains shall be melted with their blood.'

[41] With his mention of two suns, cf. Pentheus' Fury-maddened hallucination (*Aen.* 4.470).

[42] *Anat. of mel.* 3.2.2.1. On kinds of melancholy affecting different faculties and forming grades of inner experience, see Klibansky, esp. 358–9.

between the invocations of witnesses to the shepherds' grief. But the trios of invocations turn out to have no simple relation. How do goatherd gods relate to Mercury? Kalstone's schematic contrast ('gods of the earth . . . gods of the heavens') may be accepted as a first crude approximation. Strephon's nymphs, at most followers of Diana, were very minor deities, not necessarily even immortal; and his satyrs were demigods, mere goat-haired men. 'Goatherd *gods*', however, draws attention to the lascivious satyrs' confused connection with *fauni* and *panes*. Klaius certainly appeals to witnesses of a higher court: he has his eye on the heavens and the moral heights. But it is too simple to call Strephon's amorousness earthbound; he too, after all, loves Venus Urania.

Behind Strephon's invocations lies a pagan source, Lucretius' disquisition on echoes (*De rerum nat.* 4.570–94). There goat-footed satyrs, nymphs and fauns occur together as the legendary haunters of places with echoes, associated with the music of the goatherd god Pan.[43] Pan, who was often identified with Faunus, might lead nymphs and satyrs; and his brute attributes might denote the earth; but his upper parts touched heaven, and his hairs were the rays of celestial bodies. Pan (or Nature) was Mercury's son, so that Sidney aptly makes it the younger shepherd Strephon who invokes the *panes*, and the older pastor Klaius who answers with an invocation of Mercury himself, the Logos from which Nature issues.[44] Lucretius describes echoes as 'six- or seven-fold', so that Sidney's Echo, 'tired in secret forests' by the music of the shepherds, mythologizes the sestina's form. But she also belongs here as one of Pan's few amours. Although like Faunus he was *nympharum fugientum amator*,[45] Pan had not many reported loves: only

---

[43] 'I have observed places tossing back 6 or 7 utterances when you have launched a single one. . . . These places are haunted by goat-footed satyrs and by nymphs. Tales are told of fauns . . . of twanging lyre-strings and plaintive melodies poured out by flutes . . . of music far-heard by the country-folk when Pan . . . runs his arched lips again and again along the wide-mouthed reeds, so that the pipe's wildwood rhapsody flows on unbroken': Lucretius *On the Nature of the Universe* tr. R. Latham (Harmondsworth 1957) 148.

[44] For these interpretations see F. Bacon *De sapientia veterum* ch. 6, expanded in *De augmentis scientiarum* ch. 13; and cf. N. Conti *Mythologiae* 5.6 (Lyons 1653, pp. 452–3).

[45] Horace *Odes* 3.18.1, of Faunus. Faunus became an emblem of lust: see e.g. A. Alciati *Emblemata* (Lyons 1600) Embl. 72, p. 273; Ripa (1603) 295. His close association with Sylvanus, Pan and the satyrs in Renaissance dictionaries is discussed in Starnes and Talbert 80.

Echo, Diana (whose captivation came to be interpreted as a cosmogonic myth) and Syrinx. The nymph Syrinx escaped by metamorphosis into a reed, from which Pan, himself a 'finder-out of music', made the pipe Lucretius refers to. Both seven-reeded pipe and seven-fold Echo were interpreted by Renaissance mythologists as symbols of the cosmic harmony of seven planetary spheres.[46] Thus when Strephon curses the inventors of music, he curses nothing less than the created order itself; just as when, at *Lamon's Tale* line 520, he breaks his pipe.

Mercury, whom Klaius invokes, was also an inventor of music. He invented the lyre, and so could accurately be described as a '*fiddling* finder-out of music' (the lyre being often thought of as a bowed instrument).[47] Needless to say the seven strings of this lyre, too, symbolized the music of the spheres. But Mercury's music was of a higher order, as the contest between Pan and Apollo showed. In that contest, which could be allegorized as one between human and divine orderings of nature, Apollo used Mercury's lyre.[48] And Mercury matched—or out-matched—Pan in other ways. As *Hermes Charidotes* he led the nymphs in dance and was worshipped as a shepherd god:[49] as *divinus amator* he raised the mind above terrestrial love to the heavens: [50] and as *psychopompos* he guided spirits through death to a world beyond nature.[51] Hence he is 'foregoer to the evening' here because he shows the way into the 'mortal . . . evening' (l. 42) of death.[52] The

[46] See Conti 5.6; p.454: 'Fama est praeterea Echo fuisse a Pane amatam, quippe cum coelorum harmoniam Echo esse putarent, quae redundaret e ratione motuum. Atque ad septem planetarum imitationem septem chordarum instrumenta musica prius fuerunt inventa. . . . Pan igitur . . . creditur septem calamorum concinne inter se connexorum fistulam excogitasse'; also G. Zarlino *Institutioni harmoniche* (Venice 1573) 21, cit. E. Winternitz *Musical Instruments and their Symbolism in Western Art* (1967) 200n.; cf. below, p.77 and n.67.

[47] cf. *Lira da braccia, Lira da sette corde*. It was the commonest bowed instrument in late medieval religious art (Winternitz ch. 5). On its invention by Mercury see ibid. 200n. and Conti 5.5 (p.438).

[48] Bacon loc. cit. n.44 above. Contrast Sannazaro's less cosmological Syrinx myth of the origin of pastoral poetry (Kalstone 37).

[49] One type of votive relief associated this Hermes with Pan; see J. Harrison *Prolegomena to the Study of Greek Religion* (New York 1957) 291. Conti 436–7 traces his shepherd cult to the stealing of Admetus' oxen.

[50] See Wind 124. A. Bochi *Symbolicae quaestiones* (Bologna 1574) *Symbolum* 143, where Mercury aflame contemplates the heavens, might gloss Klaius' inward fire at l. 56.   [51] Wind 121, 124; cf. *Aen.* 4.244.

[52] cf. Petrarch *Canzoniere* 237.7 'Di di in di spero omai l'ultima sera'. For Mercury associated with night cf. René King of Naples *Oeuvres complètes* ed. de Quatrebarbes (Angers 1845) 4.187.

thought continues into Klaius' third invocation, which is as closely linked with his first as Strephon's satyrs with his *panes*. Whereas he particularizes the evening planet as Mercury, he evasively calls the morning star 'lovely star, entitled of the morning', thus implying the connection between evening and morning stars, which was often applied as a symbol of the resurrection.[53] Klaius' invocations have in fact a Christian source, *Anticlaudianus* 2.3, where the reciprocation of Mercury and the morning star Lucifer, together with the phases of Phoebe, are instances of God's mysterious laws.[54] Pastor Klaius seeks Christian consolation, it seems.

In keeping with this view, Klaius' music, the music that he himself brings into being (l. 21), is nothing less than a harmony of the passions. Where Strephon offers the gods his 'woes' (l. 5), Klaius offers his 'voice' (l. 10), in articulate complaint. As their Greek-derived names suggest, Strephon suffers, whereas Klaius weeps, making both their complaints, by the concord of his echo, harmonious.[55] It is he who makes their music that of moral and psychological integration. Of this ideal, frequently encountered in Renaissance literature and thought, *Ye goatherd gods* constitutes, indeed, one of the finest expressions.[56] Pico had taken the Pythagorean theory of the soul to imply an octave proportion, 2:1, between the rational and concupiscible faculties. And this same harmony appears, over and over again, as a formal pattern in Sidney's poem. Both sets of invocations have the proportion 2:1 between male and female invocatees, respectively. So has the distribution of mentions of the sun between Strephon and

[53] The two could even be identified: see *The Poems of John Milton* ed. J. Carey and A. Fowler (1968) 683–4, n. to *Par. Lost* 5.166–70.
[54] Alan of Lille *Anticlaudianus* 2.3, Migne *P.L.* 210.501; tr. Cornog 68: 'By what law they go, joined in what compact, Lucifer and Cyllenius . . . and alternate turns at duty. . . . They give themselves reciprocal names; Hesperus accompanies the setting, Lucifer the rising. In what manner the moon begs an alien beauty. . . .' cf. ibid. 4.6, Migne *P.L.* 210.527, Cornog 100–1. Alan's ref. to the siren who follows the shepherd-sun into evening ('totusque senescit/ vespere . . ./ hunc cantum Syrena parit, quae Solis adhaeret/ motibus') makes one wonder if Sidney's editors have been hasty in rejecting the *mortal siren of an evening* of many good MSS, and in preferring *serene* (a rarer word, but doubtful metrically).
[55] *Strephon* from στρέφω = torture (cf. Plato *Rep.* 330E 'torment the soul'); *Klaius* from κλαίω = lament. See Ringler 382.
[56] The most elaborate is surely A. Kircher *Musurgia* (Rome 1650): see J. Hollander *The Untuning of the Sky: Ideas of Music in English Poetry 1500–1700* (Princeton, N.J. 1961); and Fowler *Numbers of Time* 268–83.

Klaius.[57] Again, lines regretting lost peace maintain intelligible proportions with lines expressive of present suffering. Throughout stanzas 1–4 and 7–8 the balance is scrupulously maintained, though arrangements of 'good' and 'bad' lines vary.[58] Stanzas 5–6 and 9–10 present only suffering. But the final pair of stanzas, 11 and 12, have good and bad lines in octave proportion, 4:2. A similar meaning underlies the arrangement of players in the Barley-break game in *Lamon's Tale*, whose relation to *Ye goatherd gods* we must now consider.

"Lamon's Tale".

The 1593 *Arcadia* assigns to Lamon (who also recounts *Ye goatherd gods* in that and in the 1590 edition) an incomplete narrative pastoral relating an early episode in the love of Strephon and Klaius for Urania. Ringler (p. 494) argues that Sidney never intended it to be included in *Arcadia*. But as we shall see *Lamon's Tale* has a structural connection with the sestina form of *Ye goatherd gods*, which on Ringler's assumption might not be easy to account for.

The first half of *Lamon's Tale* shows virtue-loving Klaius and the at first 'lickorous' Strephon falling in love with a humble yet Venus-like Urania.[59] But the remainder, lines 207–416, is devoted to an account of a barley-break game, whose length hardly seems justified by occasional darts of satire on courtly life.[60] Justification, if it was ever possible, may be impossible now. Perhaps we have simply to own to a lack of feeling for this innocent sort of narrative. Still, there are allowances to be made. Our patience with trivial natural detail in Romantic poetry depends on the hope that it may turn out to be expressive of the poet's sentiments; whereas we tend to assume that only the most minimal signs of mental life can ever have accompanied descriptions of games, dancing and other ritualized Eliza-

---

[57] Stanzas 3, 8, 9, 11 (*bis*) and 12, i.e., 4 in Strephon's stanzas, 2 in Klaius'. Contrast *Is.* 30.26: 'the light of the sun shall be seven-fold . . . in the day that the Lord bindeth up the breach of his people'.
[58] If g = a 'good' line, b a 'bad' line, sts 1–4 have the form $gggbbb$; St.7 $gbgbgb$; and st.8 $bgbggb$.
[59] Klaius' device is a Column of Virtue, emblem of freedom from 'passions' moan' (71) whereas Strephon is 'fond . . . lickerous, poisoned' (163–5). ('Lickerous', however, means 'eager for pleasure' rather than 'lecherous': *OED* s.v. *Lickerous* 2 b). Urania's sparrow is an attribute of Venus; her breast recalls 'the bowls of Venus' (99); her flight resembles that of 'Venus' bird' (353).
[60] *Pace* W.R.Davis *A Map of Arcadia* (New Haven and London 1965) 93–4.

bethan activities. Study of the philosophical *ballet de cour* of the period may help to correct this tendency.[61] So may a glance at John Davies' *Orchestra*, or the opening of Arbeau's *Orchesography*, or one of the numerous Renaissance treatises on decorum of gesture, ceremonial, or iconology. To an Elizabethan, patterns of physical movement might be fraught with deep moral and philosophical significance. It may not be over-finical, therefore, to follow the moves in Urania's barley-break game.

The 6 players are arranged in 3 pairs.[62] Of these, the 2 outer pairs try to change partners, while the pair in the middle position, 'hell', try to catch them. Players who are caught change places with the pair in hell 'till all do taste of shame' (l. 232). The particular game described by Lamon has several phases, each involving a full permutation of players (see table 3). The third phase is irregular, since Pas fails to move from his end, so that 'three did together idly stay'.[63]

Table 3

	Initial Arrangement	Final Arrangement
BARLEY-BREAK 1:	1 Strephon & 2 Urania	6 Cosma & 1 Strephon
Lines 242–65	3 Pas & 4 Nous—	5 Geron & 2 Urania—
	in hell	in hell
	5 Geron & 6 Cosma	4 Nous & 3 Pas
BARLEY-BREAK 2:	1 Cosma & 2 Strephon	6 Pas & 1 Cosma
Lines 266–316	3 Geron & 4 Urania—	5 Nous & 2 Strephon—
	in hell	in hell
	5 Nous & 6 Pas	4 Urania & 3 Geron

Strephon, however, outruns Nous and breaks with her. He pursues Urania on his own, but only catches her when Klaius enters the game and 'happy then embrace / Virtue's proof, fortune's victor, beauty's place' (l. 392). The permutations having thus arrived at 2 groups of 3, the game breaks off.

It is easy to see a resemblance between these permutations of players and the permutations of sestina endwords. According to the notation used above, the sestina rule is twice followed, players numbered 1, 2 | 3, 4 | 5, 6 moving in each case to the array 6, 1 | 5, 2 | 4, 3. There is even a simulation of the *congedo* arrangement, in the

[61] See M. M. MacGowan *L'art du ballet de cour en France, 1581–1643* (Paris 1963); F. A. Yates *The French Academies of the Sixteenth Century* (1947) 248–9 and Index s.v. *Dance, the, philosophical and religious meanings of.*
[62] *Lamon's Tale* 225–30; ed. Ringler 248.
[63] Line 329. The third phase occupies 100 lines (316–416), the others 50 apiece–another 2:1 octave proportion.

third barley-break. Mathematically, this demonstration is of course inconclusive, since the poem specifies no order within pairs. We can only say that the sequences of play are compatible with the sestina rule. Still, the connection gives one possible reason for the detail of the description. Another lies in the many hints at a cosmic significance. We are told with some astrological particularity that the game was played during the sun's first entry into Leo: that is, at the point of transition between the lunar signs, which lie behind, and the solar, which lie ahead.[64] The pairing of solar and lunar signs follows a pattern that, as we earlier conjectured, may once have explained the sestina rule.[65] At the same time—particularly in the Platonic context established by the players' names—the permutational movements may also recall the *choresis* or cosmic dance.[66]

For we may agree with Walter Davis, to whom the names of the female players 'suggest that the Plotinian hypostases are involved, and except for the puzzling rejection of *Nous* the game presents a reasonably consistent allegory of the circular operation of love.'[67] Possibly Cosma is meant to personify the sensible world (κόσμος), Nous the Intelligence of the universe, and Venus Urania the One True Fair. Davis's citation of Bernard Silvestris farther directs us to the Christian Platonic world of the *De mundi universitate* and Alan of Lille's *Anticlaudianus*, where Nous is one of the abstractions that cooperate to form an ideal character. Of Natura's composite new man in the *Anticlaudianus* a chief opponent is Old Age, 'powerful in debility, robust in ailment'.[68] This imaginative conception, which Spenser's Maleger will later develop, has perhaps a homely Arcadian counterpart in Geron (γέρων=Old Man), a sly player shunned by 'Cosma true' and elsewhere treated contemptuously by Philisides himself.[69]

---

[64] Lines 205–6: 'one fair even an hour ere Sun did rest,/ Who then in Lion's cave did enter first'. 1590 *Arcadia* begins at another astronomical transition, 'the time . . . that the Sun running a most even course becomes an indifferent arbiter between the night and the day'.

[65] See above, 40–1.

[66] Contrast Sir J. Suckling's barley-break, with its moral context, indicated by the names Love, Reason, Hate, Folly, Fancy, Pride: *Non-dramatic Works* ed. T. Clayton (Oxford 1971) 18–19.

[67] *A Map of Arcadia* 94. Other parts of the *Arcadia* may also have a Neoplatonic doctrinal content: see D. P. Walker *The Ancient Theology* (1972) ch. 4.

[68] *Anticlaudianus* 9.4; tr. Cornog 154.

[69] *Lamon's Tale* 255 ff. and 325–6; *Old Arcadia* 1st Eclogues, ed. Robertson 75. Geron is revengeful in 1590 *Arcadia* 1st Eclogues (ed. Feuillerat 137). Cosma

Sidney's philosophical game characteristically asks to be under-stood in terms of a moral and psychological, as well as a metaphysical, Platonism. Its 'hell' is unrealized desire 'which made . . . Strephon think himself in hell' (l. 540). This is particularly clear when Pas (Pan, Nature), tricked into a Fall by Geron (the Old Man of fallen human nature in Pauline theology), becomes 'mad with fall, and madder with the shame'.[70] He rushes concupiscently—in 'mad haste'—after the appearances of Cosma, only to receive a rebuff, with the advice to 'become more wise' (ll. 269–75). And his rule-breaking failure to give up Cosma for Urania contributes to the breakup of the game (ll. 327–8). If an allegory of the descent of the soul is traceable at all, it will have to be a much Christianized ver-sion. In Barley-break 1, Strephon exchanges Urania for Cosma, thus descending to the phenomenal world. But in Barley-break 2, when, drawn by his love of Urania, he joins with Nous and the principle of Intelligence, it is to find himself in hell. Indeed Nous puts him in the wrong: 'it was no right; for his default/ . . . that she should go to hell' (ll. 314–15); a sentiment without sense to the strict Neopla-tonist. Strephon's subsequent 'puzzling rejection of Nous', as Davis puts it, seems at first even more inconsistent with the Neoplatonic system. However, the various divisions of the soul into three or two by Plotinus and other Neoplatonists may incline us to associate Strephon with the lower soul.[71] His name would gain in appropriate-ness, since it was characteristic for the Plotinian lower soul, as dis-tinct from the higher, to suffer pain.[72] By the same token the virtuous Klaius may be associated with the higher soul. Or, in dy-namic terms, Strephon loves the beautiful, Klaius the good. The relation between these was for the Neoplatonist a major problem, which Plotinus attempted to solve by treating the good as superior.[73] But Sidney lays quite a different emphasis when he makes Strephon and Klaius love Urania jointly. Their simultaneous regret for a woman of 'sweetest fairness', in whom nevertheless 'the least thing that may

[70] Lines 53, 57, 141 (ed. Ringler 51–6) all identify Pas with Pan. It is a masculine form of the same word πᾶς, πᾶσα, πᾶν.   [71] Wallis 73–4.
[72] The lower soul is so defined at *Enneads* 1.4.13.5–12: see Wallis 83.
[73] ibid. 87.

---

again appears with Pas in P. Fletcher *Sicelides*, where she is 'light'; and it may be significant that an early version of Sidney's *Arcadia* calls her Hippa, the name of Dionysus' nurse (*Orph. H.* 48). For Dionysus in Plotinus' system, see R. T. Wallis *Neoplatonism* (1972) 78.

be praised . . . is her beauty' implies a not-quite-Platonic yearning for the integrated love of the 'whole man'.[74] It is for this Christian Urania, this beauty fulfilling yet surpassing the Platonic ideal, that Strephon leaves Nous behind in the metaphysical barley-break.[75]

The Arcadian Hero.

By making the 1590 *Arcadia* begin with the complaint of Strephon and Klaius, Sidney frames it in such a way as to communicate its principal themes immediately. At the same time he produces an alienation effect comparable, say, to Colin's vision of the Graces in the sixth *Faerie Queen*. I do not mean this biographically—though Strephon and Klaius are associated with Philisides (Sidney's anagrammatical persona) as the 'very born Arcadians' of the *Old Arcadia* Fourth Eclogues; and Urania has for some been the Countess of Pembroke. Nor do I refer simply to the prologue's announcement of the themes of the *Arcadia*, nor to Strephon's and Klaius' foreshadowing of Pyrochles and Musidorus,[76] nor to their contrasted ages' foreshadowing of the bitter conflict to come, between generations and their ethical codes.[77] The effect is deeper, and nearer to what Hamilton (pp. 50–1) describes: 'ironic prologue', in which *questioni d'amore* of pastoral romance conspicuously fail to prepare us for the chivalric romance that follows.

Sidney's *exordium* is more serious and personal, however, than even this suggests. For the *ianua narrandi* of the 1590 *Arcadia*, the opening of the action itself, comes when a half-dead survivor from the wreck of human society is cast ashore at the shepherds' feet. He is Pyrochles, who turns out to be a hero not unfitted for the arduous Christian world of Bernard Sylvestris or Alan of Lille. It might be concluded, therefore, that his arrival coincides with the fading of Strephon's and Klaius' world: with their loss, in fact, of Urania, who now assumes an Astraea-like mythological role, as the harmony of the spheres before

---

[74] 1590 *Arcadia* 1.1; ed. Feuillerat 7.
[75] cf. K. Duncan-Jones *RES* n.s. 17 (1966) 124, on Christian and Platonic implications of Strephon's and Klaius' being 'true runners'. However, running to grasp the love object (as Strephon does in *Lamon's Tale*) is faulted by Plotinus (*Enneads* 1.6.8). As Miss Duncan-Jones notes, Klaius' description of Urania recalls *The Song of Solomon*: with 'her eyelids are more pleasant to behold, than two white kids climbing up a fair tree' cf. *Song of Sol.* 4.2 and 5.
[76] cf. Davis 84.
[77] See K. T. Rowe *Romantic Love and Parental Authority in Sidney's 'Arcadia'* Univ. of Mich. Contribs. in Mod. Philol. 4 (Ann Arbor, Mich. 1947).

the Fall—'She, whose least word brings from the spheres their music'.[78] The Neoplatonic solution summarized in the opening episode,[79] the solution by which Astrophil also set store, has proved inadequate in the face of shipwrecked human nature. On the other hand, we should not forget that Pyrochles comes from the same sea over which Urania departed. Indeed, the hero emerges as if evoked by the shepherds' lament for the lost beauty of Urania, their 'farewell of all beauty'. No doubt he is a Christian hero inspired by the Christian Muse Urania. But he also assimilates the shepherds' aspiration to the Neoplatonic Venus Urania.[80] Klaius the Neoplatonic shepherd is after all a pastor too. We may find it touching as well as impressive that Sidney should at the same time admit the inadequacy and transience of the Neoplatonic vision, and affirm its contribution to the view he will put in its place.

We can only conclude that what seemed a pastoral lyric of simple, perhaps over-simple, content has turned out to be something very different. It would not be wholly absurd, now, to connect the morning and evening stars invoked by Klaius with those which Plotinus said were surpassed in beauty by Justice,[81] or to argue that the sestina is as much about social and cosmic order as it is about love.

Yet in its degree of seriousness *Ye goatherd gods* is not egregious. Under the husk of a similar simplicity many Elizabethan lyrics turn

[78] On the symbolism see Wind, Index s.v. *Urania*; cf. M. Rose *Heroic Love : Studies in Sidney and Spenser* (Cambridge, Mass. 1968) 44–5.
[79] See Davis 104.
[80] On the Christian Muse Urania and the divine poetry movement, see L. B. Campbell in *HLB* 8 (1935), or *Divine Poetry and Drama in Sixteenth-Century England* (Cambridge 1961); Clements ch. 3; C. D. Baker 'Certain Religious Elements in the English Doctrine of the Inspired Poet During the Renaissance' *ELH* 6 (1939); H. G. Lotspeich 'Spenser's Urania' *MLN* 50 (1935); and E. R. Curtius *European Literature and the Latin Middle Ages* tr. W. R. Trask (1953) ch. 13 and Index s.v. *Biblical Poetics*. Davis 86, a fragile argument, connects the Muse Urania with Heavenly Love and Venus Urania. The connection, however, was real: see *Geofredi Linocerii Vivariensis mythologiae Musarum libellus* ch. 9, appended to Conti, sig. Ggg 8, and cf. J. Sternberg *Untersuchungen zur Verwendung des antiken Mythus in der Dichtung Sir Philip Sidneys als ein Beitrag zur Interpretation* (Bonn 1969) 196–217, where Sidney's Urania is rightly compared to Spenser's Sapience, and (more conjecturally) interpreted as an Anteros. Duncan-Jones 130 takes Urania's departure to indicate that the *Arcadia* 'is not to be a divine but a secular work'; but it may rather mythologize the loss of harmony, of *iustitia originalis*, at the Fall, and simultaneously serve as an invocation.
[81] *Enneads* 1.6.4. Also cf. Aristotle *Nich. Ethics* 1129 b 28–9.

out to have similarly improbable, complex kernels. How far is this failure of communication on the poet's part? How far over-ingenuity on the critic's? This perennial question troubles us more and more as we come nearer to the great poetry of the late sixteenth century. It was a time when much could be communicated through encoded forms of mythology—sometimes more, sometimes less than we easily conjecture. To this we have to add the familiarity of systems such as the Neoplatonic, which may once have allowed rich implications (as in the single word *Urania*) that are now hard to recover. Hardest of all to allow for, perhaps, is the change in value whereby ceremonial activities—rituals, games and the like—which once served as symbolic 'models', have come to seem trivial or meaningless, and consequently to be neglected.

These models offer the interpreter a chance of significant new progress. As we have seen, however, they also bring new uncertainties. It is possible, for example, that the sestina rule was not consciously applied by Sidney to the Barley-break game. It occurs in so many contexts—astronomical, astrological, poetical—that it may have been felt simply as a cosmic rhythm of just compensation. The uncertainty is like that which arises with the patterns in *The garden of Cyrus*—how far did Browne 'invent' them in the modern sense, how much in the obsolete sense?

4

Spenser's
Prothalamion

═══════

The occasional character of many Elizabethan poems cuts them off from us more than we are easily aware. In all the commemorative genres—epithalamic, encomiastic, genethliac and triumphal—lack of sympathy can make us unreceptive not only to sentiments, but even to formal qualities; until we end with little idea of what we think we dislike. Spenser's *Prothalamion* is a striking instance. As a very late work, perhaps contemporary with the *Hymns*, it might be expected to have special interest. But modern critics have with few exceptions either dismissed it unappreciatively or ignored it altogether.

The Occasion.

Prothalamion had as its occasion the betrothal of two of the Earl of Worcester's daughters: Elizabeth Somerset to Henry Guldeford, Katherine to William Petre. The poem describes, though in disguised terms, a water-fête that in all likelihood actually took place. What probably happened was that the brides were rowed down the River Lee to the palace at Greenwich, then, accompanied by a following of court 'nymphs', up the Thames to Essex House (sts 7–8). There they were received at the river side by the bridegrooms and by Essex himself, with a great following. And there, at the appointed time, they celebrated their spousals or betrothals.[1] Betrothals, not weddings; therefore prothalamion, not epithalamium.[2] The double

[1] The venue may be explained by Essex's family connection with the countess and friendship with Worcester: see D. S. Norton 'Queen Elizabeth's "Bridal Day"' *MLQ* 5 (1944) 149–50 and *The Background of Spenser's 'Prothalamion'* (Princeton Univ. Doct. Thesis P.685.1940.38) 72. The reconstruction of the journey is that of Norton, the Variorum eds, and D. H. Woodward in *ELH* 29 (1962) 38.

[2] The term *prothalamion* may be Spenser's invention. But it denoted an existing genre: see Norton *Background* 8 ff., Variorum *Minor Poems* 2.664. On the epithalamic genre in general consult V. Tufte *The Poetry of Marriage*

wedding was subsequently solemnized on Monday 8 November 1596. But about the betrothals our information remains more vague. They took place in the late summer or early autumn of the same year, on a date when the bridal day was 'not long'. (Since Essex did not come to court after his Cadiz victory until 11 August, and since the court left Greenwich on 1 October, the betrothal date almost certainly fell between these *termini*.[3]) The 'real time' of the poem has also a two-fold character. From one point of view the spousal fête is remembered at some subsequent time; from another, the weddings are expected and even anticipated in a song (st. 6). *Prothalamion* plays around the two occasions, as if to weave them together and accomplish the weary time between.

Every aspect of the poem is involved with the historical events. Externally, it forms a part of the social protocol, perhaps actually being intended as a gift to the brides.[4] Formally, it honours the occasion by commemorating, so that Spenser constructed it monumentally, in ways to be discussed later, with appropriate temporal proportions. And substantively its statement is in the mode of personal compliment and allusion, taking up actual circumstances and accepting them as the terms of communication. Many features were almost predetermined. A double betrothal set particular conditions; and the ostensible sentiments, at least, could hardly range very far—'here fits not well/Old woes but joys to tell.' Moreover, some politeness of tone was obligatory in such a commissioned work: a feature that has counted against it in recent estimates. (Commendations of noble lords are now thought sycophantic unless the poet in question is Shakespeare.) It is as if we ourselves preferred wedding guests to be rude, or speeches at wedding receptions to be confined to expressions of moderate approbation.[5] A favourably-disposed critic, on the other

[3] Norton *Background* 85–7. Essex's engagements, and correspondence relating to the betrothal, limit the probable date to 7–29 Sept.
[4] From Essex, suggests Norton ibid. 92.
[5] On the panegyric mode, including far more extreme instances than Spenser's, see B. K. Lewalski *Donne's 'Anniversaries' and the Poetry of Praise* (Princeton, N.J. 1973); O. B. Hardison *The Enduring Monument* (Chapel Hill, N.C. 1962); R. Nevo *The Dial of Virtue* (Princeton, N.J. 1963); J. Kinsley 'Dryden and the Art of Praise' *Essential Articles for the Study of John Dryden* ed. H. T. Swedenberg (1966) 541–50.

(Los Angeles 1969). On Elizabethan spousal ceremonies see Norton ibid. 10–39, esp. 14 on spousals *de praesenti* and *de futuro*; also H. Swinburne *A treatise of spousals or matrimonial contracts* (1686) 219–20.

hand, may in the present moral climate be so anxious to demonstrate the poem's acceptably modern stance that he dwells on its element of personal complaint, and treats its compliments as ironic or cynical or wryly practical—or anything, but sincere.[6] We are reluctant to allow that Spenser may have embraced a public occasion.

An occasional lyric such as this invites misinterpretation, because the critic would otherwise be at a loss. Not that the case of *Prothalamion* is really so open-and-shut as to need only verdict and sentence. But the poem seems to have few obscurities, tensions, or difficult images. Throughout stanzas 2–7, indeed, the usual *points d'appui* of textual analysis are so lacking that criticism passes over them altogether.[7] It has concentrated instead on delicacies of tone, particularly in the concluding stanzas. But perhaps it is premature to form a view of these, before determining what formal decorums may affect them. To begin with, we need to know just what the ostensible compliment is, and what conventional forms its organization takes, however unpromising their surface simplicities, however alien their inward complexities.

Poetic Garlands.

Prothalamion's most off-putting *simplesse* comes in its floral passages, which critics easily see as having a vacuous early-Tennysonian decorativeness. The lines on little wicker baskets, for example, have been described as of 'extraordinary feebleness'.[8] Much of the poem goes in flower gathering and flower arrangement; yet these operations are not now attended to very carefully—perhaps because sensuous detail is absent from the flowers, which as Elton said 'Spenser does not watch intently, but seems to choose for the melody of their names'.[9] But the flowers of lyric can be significant in more ways than Elton—or perhaps even Imlac—realized.

A meadow by the Thames is adorned with flowers and buds (st. 1). Here nymphs gather flowers of various species in separate individual wicker baskets, and transfer them to a large flasket for composition into bridegrooms' posies (st. 2). Then the two swan-brides arrive: these are bombarded with flowers, which strew the water (st. 5). Meanwhile two of the nymphs bind flowers into

---

[6] H. Berger, e.g., says of sts 6 and 9 that 'their rhetoric smacks of the professional performance': see *EC* 15 (1965) 375.
[7] A distinguished exception is Woodward.
[8] By J. N. Smith in an otherwise valuable contribution, *RES* n.s. 10 (1959) 173–8.   [9] *Variorum Minor Poems* 2.497.

garlands and present them to the brides—a coronation simultaneous with the singing of an inset spousal song in stanza 6. This is certainly ornamental; but it is very far from being merely decorative verbal embroidery, routine poetic brocade. Indeed a flower ritual very like this may actually have taken place; for in Spenser's age (and until quite recently) people found time to make garlands and posies. At annual festivals they regularly decorated churches with garlands,[10] and they would often present garlands, symbolic of honour, both to public figures and private individuals.[11] Our own congratulatory bouquets, posies at weddings, wreaths at funerals and Christmas decorations are attenuated forms of practices once more widespread and more consciously symbolic.

The flower-gathering has also a mythological dimension. Coming as they do after the Zephyrus of stanza 1, these nymphs with 'greenish locks' obviously realize Ovid's myth of Flora. The nymph Chloris (The Green One) was wandering in spring when Zephyrus pursued and took her. But he made up for his violence by giving her the name of bride (*nomina nuptae*) and changing her dower fields into a fruitful garden. Now called Flora, she was queen of innumerable flowers: 'As soon as the varied foliage is warmed by the sunbeams, the Hours assemble, clad in painted weeds, and cull my gifts in light baskets. At once the Graces draw near, and twine garlands and wreaths to bind their celestial hair.'[12] More fleetingly, *Prothalamion* alludes to the gathering of marigolds, violets and poppies by Proserpina's maidens, just before her rape by Pluto: 'One filled baskets plaited of supple twigs ['haec implet lento calathos e vimine nexos'], another loaded her lap. . . .'.[13] It is characteristic of Spenser that on such an occasion he should introduce allusions—distant and delicate but nonetheless distinct—to these myths of rough sexual capture. He addresses the emotions of brides at the prospect of their initiations; reflecting and calming imagined fears—'Sweet breathing Zephyrus did *softly* play.'[14]

[10] See Hieatt *Short Time's Endless Monument* 20.
[11] See Tervarent s.v. *Couronne* 1 *Symbole de la victoire*, 7 *Récompenses que promet la vertu* and 11 *Attribut de l'Honneur*, cols. 125–6. Vegetius devotes a chapter of the *De re militari* to triumphal and honorific crowning.
[12] *Fasti* 5.197–220. *S.C.* April 122 Gloss is external evidence that Spenser knew the passage.
[13] *Fasti* 4.435–8; cf. Moschus 2.33–71 (flower-gathering before Europa's rape), Theocritus *Idylls* 18.32 ff. (Helen's epithalamium).
[14] Jonson *Hymenaei* 810 ff. (*Ben Jonson* ed. Herford and Simpson, 11 vols

This hint (it is hardly more) belongs to a fine but tenacious strand of sexual symbolism running through much of the floral imagery. The symbolism depends on an identification of nymphs with nature for which the Ovidian contexts provided credentials of antiquity. Thus Spenser's nymphs have 'greenish locks' because like Chloris they embody an unfulfilled state, short of fruition. And just as Ovid's *variae comae* refers indifferently to foliage and hair, so Spenser's bank 'hemmed' by the Thames and 'painted' with 'variable' flowers (stanza 1) glances at the real occupation of nymphs (needlework), and perhaps even at the Hours *pictis incinctae vestibus*, who assisted in the renewal of kind.[15] A similarly anthropomorphic *double entente* underlies 'gems,/Fit to deck maidens' bowers'. They are *buds* fit to *grace*, but also *girls* fit to *decorate*; so that the continuation 'And [fit to] crown their paramours' has a sexual, though not necessarily physiological, sense.[16] So too the bridegrooms are flowers, fit to honour the bowers of their brides and of Elizabeth England's bride (ll. 15, 170).

More specifically, the flowers gathered and composed into garlands represent personal qualities cultivated by the brides in preparation for their marriage, during their nurture in the 'sacred nursery/Of virtue'.[17] This is almost explicit with the pure and 'virgin lily' (which incidentally was apt in a spousal poem, because of its prominence in the paradigmatic epithalamium, the *Song of Solomon*). But it is hardly less unambiguous with the 'primrose true', a common true-love emblem, familiar to us from Donne's *The primrose*. The other flowers have a wealth of possible meanings, from which our ignorance of

[15] *Fasti* 5.217; cf. 5.222 'unius tellus ante coloris erat'.
[16] In spite of the standard sexual *double entente* (e.g. *Hudibras* 2.1.378 'He hung a garland on his engine'). For *gem* = 'bud' see *OED* s.v. *Gem* sb. 4. Application to people was common: see ibid. 2.
[17] On flowers as soul-implanted virtues see Wind *Pagan Mysteries* 268 n.; on schematic gardens of virtues, Tuve *Allegorical Imagery* 22–4. Emblematic tapestries of flower-picking and coronet-making were common in the Middle Ages. One, Cloisters Coll. 59.85, is discussed in B. Young 'The Lady Honour and Her Children' *Metropolitan Mus. Bull.* (June 1963) 340–8.

(Oxford 1925–52) 7.236–7) uses similar imagery to assuage similar anxieties. Truth urges virgins to yield to Hymen; Opinion prefers their continuance, like flowers 'bruised with no ploughs', uncropped by 'cruel hand'. Cf. Spenser *Epith.* 190, where Medusa's severed head hints at masculine fears.

Spenser's idiolect makes it hard to select with confidence. 'Violet *pallid* blue' uses the same obscure, but probably erotic, epithet as Virgil *Eclogues* 2.47; or it may allude to the flowers gathered in baskets for Amyntas, as a pledge of love: 'Violet is for faithfulness,/ Which in me shall abide'.[18] 'Store of vermeil roses' might imply evanescent beauty, or ardent love, or even obedience.[19]

Besides these emblematic implications there may be an underlying philosophical sense. The fable of Zephyrus and Chloris was given a Neoplatonic interpretation, as Edgar Wind has shown in connection with Botticelli's *La Primavera*, and although *Prothalamion* is far from being a doctrinal poem, it may reflect Spenser's usual interest in cosmic myths of love: 'the progression Zephyr–Chloris–Flora spells out the familiar dialectic of love: Pulchritudo arises from a *discordia concors* between Castitas and Amor; the fleeing nymph and the amorous Zephyr unite in the beauty of Flora.'[20] The seasonal progression that runs through *Prothalamion* may combine metaphysical with personal or occasional significance.

Turning to the composed garlands, we observe that two are used to crown the swan-brides while the inset spousal of stanza 6 is sung: 'Their snowy foreheads therewithal they crowned,/Whilst one did sing this lay'. These simultaneous events, crowning and singing, may be regarded as correlates for features of the actual occasion. The inset song no doubt bears the same relation to *Prothalamion* itself as the crowning to the actual garlanding of the spousal celebration. But the very common use of *garland* for 'poems' allows an additional possibility, at once simpler and subtler: namely, that the inset song

[18] *A handful of pleasant delights* (1584) ed. H.E. Rollins (New York 1965) 4. V. Rendell *Wild Flowers in Literature* (1934) 69–71, connecting the violet's erotic associations with lovers' pallor, cites Horace *Odes* 3.10.14, Shakespeare *Sonn.* 99; cf. n.81 below. On the lily of purity and *pudicitia* see Tervarent col.248; on the primrose, which sometimes signified its petals' nuptial number, see Rendell 259–60 citing Donne *The primrose* and Browne *Pastorals* 2.3.

[19] Tervarent s.v. *Rose* I *Attribut de Vénus*, cols. 323–4; contrast *A handful of pleasant delights* 5: 'Roses is to rule me / with reason as you will,/ For to be still obedient. . . .' Also cf. *S.C.* Feb. 129–32 where the Briar is 'Dyed in lily white, and crimson red,/ With leaves engrained in lusty green,/ Colours meet to clothe a maiden queen.' For lily and rose as sacred to Juno see Jonson *Hymenaei* 220 side-note *s*, ed. Herford and Simpson 7.217; and Statius *Silvae* 1.2.22.

[20] Wind *Pagan Mysteries* 117.

and the garlands both represent aspects of *Prothalamion*. Thus the presentation of garlands may refer to the presentation of *Prothalamion*'s poetic garlands as a wedding gift. The presenting and the singing would then necessarily be simultaneous, because they would be the same event. In the same way, the bridegrooms' posies (poesies) would be both verses and flowers,[21] and the mutual compliments of the prothalamion would find reflection in the reciprocal garlanding of brides and bridegrooms.

If *Prothalamion* were a composed garland or pair of five-stanza garlands, what could be meant by the separate stages of garland-making on which, as we have seen, Spenser lavishes much description? The nymphs crop the flowers, put them in individual 'little wicker baskets', transfer them to a communal flasket.[22] Now in Moschus 2.37–44, Europa's flower basket is itself a great work of art: 'a great marvel and a masterpiece of Hephaestus, given by him to Libya on the day when the Earth-shaker took her to his bed. . . . And in this basket were wrought many shining pieces of cunning work.' But in Spenser the artefacts given are garlands, not baskets. His baskets, being containers, could only correspond to features of the work's external form. Perhaps stanzas, into which the flowers of the poem's rhetoric are gathered? The flasket would denote the whole form 'filled' or implemented. Spenser's description of the baskets as 'made of fine twigs entrailed [woven] curiously' now acquires some interest. If baskets render stanzas, twigs must render lines. The metaphor would be apt, for in analysing stanza forms Elizabethan critics commonly represented lines by rules and rhyme-links by loops,[23] so that diagrams resembled basket-work:

---

[21] *Posy*, a form of *poesy*, first a motto verse (esp. for a ring), subsequently an emblem or bouquet: *OED* s.v. *Posy* sb. 1–2, exs. from 1533 and 1565. For *garland* = collection of poems, see ibid. s.v. *Garland* sb. 4, exs. from 1526. M. Drayton *Shepherd's garland* (1593) Ecl. 3 and the revised *Pastorals* (1619) Ecl. 3 bear a close relation to *Proth*. Spenser counters *Shepherd's garland* 3.95 'Go pass on Thames and hie thee fast unto the Ocean sea' with his refrain, which in turn influences *Pastorals* 3.49 'Stay Thames, to hear my song, thou great and famous flood'. See Drayton *Works* ed. J.W.Hebel et al. 5 vols (Oxford 1931–41) 1.55–9, 2.527–31.
[22] i.e., a long shallow basket: *OED* s.v. *Flasket* 1; cf. G.Fletcher *Christ's victory in heaven* st.85 'Bring, bring ye Graces all your silver flaskets'.
[23] Puttenham 2.10, ed. Willcock and Walker 88; cf. the diagram in Drayton *The barons' wars* Epist. to the Reader, ed. Hebel et al. 2.4.

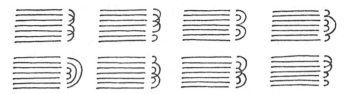

from Puttenham *The art of English poesy* 2.10

Since Spenser hints that the lines are entrailed *curiously*, we shall clearly have to attend to stanza pattern rather closely. It would be surprising if all this representation of garland-making did not give some clue to *Prothalamion*'s formal structure.

The Garlands Stellified.

Garlands or crowns are not the only images of circularity in *Prothalamion*. Its last stanza introduces the ecliptic circle, 'the baldric of the heavens'. That this is more than an incidental flourish, content and form both show. *Prothalamion*'s action, like that of many epithalamia, runs from morning (Zephyrus, blowing from the west, *'did delay/ Hot Titan's beams'*) to evening (the appearance of Hesper); while its line-total, 180, refers to the 180 degrees of the sun's daytime course round half the circle of the heavens.[24] Moreover, several prominent images have their places on the celestial globe, where the same ecliptic circle intersects and connects them. To some extent this is made explicit: Petre and Guldeford themselves are compared, not merely to Castor and Pollux (types of friendship and concord), but to Gemini 'the twins of Jove' in particular, 'Which deck the baldric of the heavens bright'.

The brides receive more complex treatment. They have the guise of swans until the last stanza, when they change from 'birds' to

[24] On numerological uses of 180 see Fowler *Triumphal Forms* 136, 144. The diurnal pattern of *Proth.* appears in such details as the 'daisy [day's eye] that at evening closes'. The circle was a favourite motif in nuptial iconology: cf., e.g., Jonson *Hymenaei* (see D.J. Gordon 'Hymenaei: Ben Jonson's Masque of Union' *JWI* 8 (1945) 120); also Swinburne *Of spousals* 207–8: 'the ring being circular, that is, round, and without end, importeth . . . that their mutual love and hearty affection should roundly flow from the one to the other, as in a circle, and that continually, and for ever.'

'brides': a metamorphosis that has been interpreted as allegory. But perhaps the swan state is a masque-like disguise, whose relinquishment in stanza 10 needs no explanation.[25] Several proprieties may be distinguished. One is rhetorical, depending on a common word-play between *bird* and *bride*.[26] Another is similarity of movement: the brides glide over the water with the stateliness of the real swans inhabiting the Thames. Moreover, the brides' barge may actually have been decorated with a swan device; since their mother's family, the Staffords, claimed descent from the Swan Knight, and bore the white swan of Mandeville and Bohun.[27] A more literary decorum links the swan-brides generically with those in the river epithalamia of Leland and Vallans, where the motif, emblematic of purity, was first established.[28] But all these decorums are not enough for Spenser, who specifically compares his swans to 'that same pair/Which through the sky draw Venus' silver team [coach]'.[29] The allusion is doubly reinforced: the swans shine 'as heaven's light'; and they excel the rest of the flock 'as Cynthia doth shend/The lesser stars'.[30] Spenser thus connects the brides with Cygnus, an extra-zodiacal constellation.

In stanza 4 the nymphs 'which now had flowers their fill' stand amazed by the swans 'their wondering eyes to fill'. The anthropomorphic half-suggestion of this *conversio*, of the moral flowers and of the Chloris-Flora allusion is strengthened by the report that the brides were bred 'In sweetest season, when each flower and weed/The earth did fresh array'. Girls in this poem seem to change freely

[25] Though J.N.Smith adduces similar swan transformations in folklore.
[26] cf. Shakespeare *Cymb.* 4.2.197, *Shrew* 5.2.46. The words were not phonetically close in 16th-cent. English, unless the earlier form of *bird*, i.e. *brid* (/brɪd/), survived beyond 1500 in dialect and was well known (unlikely). A complicating factor was confusion of *bird* with M.E. *bird* = young maiden (*OED* s.v. *Bird* 1 1 d). For the history of the 3 words I am much indebted to private information from Profs. A.McIntosh and E.J.Dobson.   [27] Norton *Background* 225 n.417.
[28] J.Leland Κύκνειον ᾆσμα. *Cygnea cantio* (1545); W.Vallans *A tale of two swans* (1590). See Variorum *Minor Poems* 2.667ff.; and n.83 below.
[29] Lines 62–3. Support for *team* = 'coach' might be found in *OED* (s.v. *Team* 11 5; but with no ex. before 1641). Probably a Latinism: cf. *temo* = Bootes' wagon. For swans as Venus' team see Cartari *Imagini delli dei* facs. ed. W.Koschatsky (Graz 1963) 342; Horace *Odes* 3.28.15, 4.1.10; Ovid *Met.* 10.717–18; Marlowe *Hero and Leander* 1.352.
[30] Lines 52, 121–2; cf. their address as 'the world's fair ornament,/ And heaven's glory' at 91–2.

into swans ('birds') and stars, while at the same time (considered as mortals) remaining flowers.[31] It is a characteristically elusive, metamorphic imagery, which fuses natural forms with a plasticity reminiscent of Ovid and predictive of Shelley. We almost wonder whether it can be coincidence that the *Almagest* and other authorities took the supposedly Arabic name of *Cygnus* to mean 'sweet-smelling as the *lily*'.[32]

Since the poem's composition seems to be symbolized by the weaving of circular forms, we may reasonably enquire whether it contains a whole garland of signs like those stellifying the brides and grooms. For zodiacs of images there was a precedent in Giles Durant's *Le zodiac amoureux*, imitated as recently as 1595 by Chapman;[33] and Spenser himself had already represented the heavens numerologically in the 24 hour-stanzas of *Epithalamion*.[34] In visual art, such astronomical schemes were common. Giulio Romano's Sala dei Venti in the Palazzo del Te is one that, like Durant's and Chapman's, introduces extra-zodiacal constellations.

This hypothesis meets with early encouragement. In the first stanza Zephyrus, the West Wind, suits the westerly sector of the ecliptic and the first sign of the spring season when he transforms the earth:[35] as Sylvester puts it, 'no sooner' does the sun go on holiday 'in pleasant inns/Of Aries, Taurus, and the gentle Twins' than 'sweet Zephyrus begins to buss his Flora'.[36] Stanza 2 with its 'flock of nymphs'

---

[31] Flowers symbolized human frailty: see Valeriano *Hieroglyphica* 55.1, p.683 on *imbecillitas humana*.

[32] The *Almagest* of 1515 has '*Eurisim* quasi redolens ut lilium', the *Alfonsine Tables* of 1521 '*Hyresym* et dicitur quasi redolens ut lilium ab ireo [iris]'. See R. H. Allen *Star Names* (New York 1963) 194; G.-B. Riccioli *Almagestum novum* tom. I, pt I (Bologna 1651) 406.

[33] *Ovid's banquet of sense: a coronet for his mistress Philosophy*; P. B. Bartlett (ed.) *The Poems of George Chapman* (New York 1962) 87–92. See Fowler *Triumphal Forms* 140–6, 208–14.

[34] 1595; see Hieatt *Short Time's Endless Monument* and 'The Daughters of Horus', *Form and Convention in the Poetry of Edmund Spenser* ed. W. Nelson (New York and London 1961) 103–21; Fowler *Triumphal Forms* 161–73. Other instances of astronomical numerology are mentioned ibid. 133–97.

[35] In the myth discussed above (Ovid *Met.* 1.107–8, *Fasti* 5.197; Wind *Pagan Mysteries* 115 ff.). Zephyrus was often associated with 'temperate' Aries, the most W. sign: e.g. Sylvester's *Du Bartas* 368.

[36] ibid. 108–9. According to Harvey, Spenser had this Day of the *Divine weeks* by heart (*Gabriel Harvey's Marginalia* ed. G. C. M. Smith (Stratford-Upon-Avon 1913) 161).

(described only here, though mentioned elsewhere) matches Taurus, which was characterized by Manilius as 'rich in maidens' because the Hyades and Pleiades forming part of the constellation were mythologically daughters of Atlas.[37] The flower-picking in this stanza is also appropriate seasonally, being an Occupation of April.[38] The third stanza continues the zodiac by dwelling on Leda: Gemini was *Ledaeum sidus*, Dante's 'lovely nest of Leda' (*Par.* 27.98) and Cowley's 'Ledaean stars'. The fourth stanza brings the 'summer's heat' of the solstitial sign Cancer. And stanza 5's garland-binding and crowning accords with the constellation Corona, whose setting Spenser himself connects with Leo in *The shepherd's calendar*:

> And now the sun hath reared up
>   his fieryfooted team,
> Making his way between the Cup,
>   and golden Diadem:
> The rampant Lion hunts he fast. . . .[39]

[37] Manilius *Astron.* 4.521; the Pleiades were often called a *flock* of birds (Allen 394–5). I. Sacrobosco *De sphaera* 9, comm. Robertus Anglicus (*The 'Sphere' of Sacrobosco and Its Commentators* ed. L. Thorndike (Chicago 1949) 224) takes Virgil *Georg.* 1.221–2—'ante tibi Eoae Atlantides abscondantur/ Gnosiaque ardentis decedat stella Coronae'—to mean the cosmic setting of the Pleiades with Taurus, 'opposite to Scorpio'. For reliable brief accounts of the astrological system, see W. Hartner 'The Mercury Horoscope of Marcantonio Michiel of Venice' in *Oriens-Occidens* (Hildesheim 1968) 440–95 and J. D. North '"Kalenderes enlumyned ben they": Some Astronomical Themes in Chaucer' *RES* n.s. 20 (1969) 129–54. F. Boll *Sphaera* (Leipzig 1903); F. Boll and C. Bezold *Sternglaube und Sterndeutung* (Leipzig and Berlin 1931); and R. Eisler *The Royal Art of Astrology* (1946) provide fuller treatments.

[38] cf. *S.C.* April, whose relation with *Proth.* has been remarked. For flower bearing as April's symbol see É. Mâle *The Gothic Image* tr. D. Nussey (1961) 71–2 and J. C. Webster *The Labours of the Months* (New York 1970) esp. 90, 102–3 (mythological implications) and 175–9 (statistics showing this representation in 31 of 43 12th-cent. exs.). Later exs. are common: cf. *Queen Mary's Psalter* B.L. Royal MS 2 B.vii fol. 74b (14th cent.).

[39] July 17–21, a difficult passage: though Corona borealis and Crater straddle the sun's ecliptic path, neither was in the July sign Leo. (Crater was in Virgo, Corona in Libra.) Spenser follows an astrological schematic tradition such as Manilius' or Firmicus Maternus', giving *paranatellonta* or constellations that rise or set with the signs. Thus Hyginus *Poet. astron.* 3.4 connects Corona's setting with Leo's rising. According to Firmicus 8.10 and 8.11 Corona rises in 5° of Virgo, the sign to which precession had moved Leo by Spenser's time. Corona had moved too; but concerning extra-zodiacal constellations Firmicus had the authority of literary tradition: cf.

Virgo appears in stanza 6 as Peace, a common form of the constellation: here 'endless Peace', one of the powers invoked in the inset
wedding song.[40] The first six stanzas thus have matter consonant
with a half-zodiac that would run *Aries | Taurus | Gemini | Cancer | Leo |
Virgo.*

These are not, however, the only stellar images. In stanza 1
'dainty gems,/Fit to . . . crown their paramours' rather precisely
indicates Corona borealis, the stellified wedding crown originally
given by Bacchus to Ariadne. Ovid's account of its metamorphosis—
'gemmae nitidos vertuntur in ignes'—has the same ambiguity between gems and buds.[41] (The celestial crown was so regularly a
floral wreath that according to Manilius those born under Ariadne's
crown will be makers of nosegays and festoons.[42]) The connection
between Corona borealis and Aries, the zodiacal sign of stanza 1,
depends on a Roman and medieval convention whereby constellations were ordered by their risings and settings, often with respect
to an opposite sign. Thus Ovid *Fasti* 3.459 assigns 'the Cnossian
crown' to March. In any correct reckoning of cosmical or acronychal
risings or settings, of course, latitude and ascension would have to be
taken into account: we cannot assume that because Aries is setting

[40] On Virgo identified with olive-bearing Eirene or Pax, see Ripa 375,
Cartari 168, Allen 462.

[41] ibid. 178 discusses *Gemma coronae* as a constellation name. Predictably, the
ambiguity disgusted Joseph Spence (*Polymetis* (1747) 165, on Ovid *Met.*
8.180).

[42] Manilius *Astron.* 5.254 ff., tr. T. Creech (1697) 65: 'Next shines the Maid,
and when the Maid ascends/ Thrice five degrees, the glorious Crown
attends./ . . . They give soft arts, for here the Virgin shines,/ And there the
Virgin's Crown, and each combines/ Soft beams agreeing in the same
designs./ Birth influenced then shall raise fine beds of flowers,/ And twine
their creeping jasmine round their bowers;/ The lilies, violets in banks
dispose,/ The purple poppy, and the blushing rose [*Pallenteis violas, et
purpureos hyacinthos,/ Liliaque, et Tyrias imitata papavera luces,/ Vernantisque
rosae rubicundo sanguine florem*]:/ For pleasure shades their rising mounts
shall yield,/ And real figures paint the gaudy field:/ Or they shall wreath
their flowers, their sweets entwine,/ To grace their mistress . . . .' For floral
crowns in the ancient wedding ceremony, see Scaliger *Poetice* 3.101
'Epithalamion' 152 D ad fin.

the Sala dei Venti programme, in which Corona was still connected with
Virgo (E. H. Gombrich *Symbolic Images* (1972) 111 and pl. 113). Spenser's
'calendar for every year' may even assume a poetical astronomy with constellations occupying their ancient positions.

Libra (and Corona) are rising. However, as Sacrobosco's authoritative *De sphaera* explained, 'the risings and settings of the signs are taken in two ways, according to the [ancient] poets and according to the astronomers'. In the former system latitude is ignored, so that, for example, 'cosmic setting is a matter of opposition'.[43] Spenser very probably knew the *De sphaera*; and in any case would be familiar with the convention, from the ancient poets on whom Sacrobosco drew, and from Chaucer, who uses it in *The legend of good women*. There the constellation in question, as it happens, is Corona: 'And in the signe of Taurus men may se/The stones of hire corone shyne clere.'[44] J.S.P. Tatlock, who first explained the Chaucerian passage, gave several late medieval examples of the 'opposite sign' convention; these, together with the wide influence of the looser Manilian tradition in the Renaissance, argue continued currency after the age of Chaucer.[45] We have to think of a simplified and inaccurate poetical astronomy, in which settings are by same or opposite signs, or by authority of the ancient poets. We may consequently expect signs and constellations to be identified.[46]

The other stellar images in *Prothalamion* now fall into place. Sagittarius the domicile of 'Jove', in stanza 3, is opposite Gemini. Cygnus, which as we have seen appears mythologically in stanza 4, lies opposite

[43] *De sphaera* 3, ed. Thorndike 95, 129–30: 'Occasus vero cosmicus est ratione oppositionis, quando sol oritur cum aliquo signo cuius signi oppositum occidit cosmice. . . . sole existente in Scorpione, que cum oritur cum sole, Taurus ubi sunt Pleiades occidit.' Later Sacrobosco considers rising and setting 'according to the astronomers' and only then introduces latitude, oblique ascension, etc. The evening setting of Corona borealis on 9 Nov., the day after the wedding (e.g. Riccioli 1.469), may have influenced Spenser's design.
[44] *L.G.W.* 2223–4. J.S.P. Tatlock in *MLN* 29 (1914) 100–1 correctly identifies the phenomenon, without however supplying a medieval astronomical context.
[45] e.g. in Pontanus; see Gombrich 225 n.5.
[46] The movement of the constellations was more widely known in Elizabethan times, but rarely acknowledged in literature. (An exception is *F.Q.* 5 Proem, discussed Fowler *Numbers of Time* 192–4.) It suited writers to adhere to the familiar unvarying model of 'the poets'. Thus they would assign March to Aries, without specifying sign (sector of the heavens) as against constellation. The details of this schematic model could easily be drawn from *auctores*, globe, or star map, without need for calculation. On Spenser's limitations in this regard, see *Harvey's Marginalia* ed. Smith 162: 'Pudet ipsum Spenserum, etsi sphaerae, astrolabiique non plane ignarum; suae in astronomicis canonibus, tabulis, instrumentisque imperitiae.'

Cancer.[47] And stanza 6 (Virgo) aptly alludes to Pisces, under its ancient name *Venus et Cupido*,[48] in the invocation to 'Venus, that is queen of love,/With her heart-quelling son'. The spousal song of stanza 6 completes a sketchy zodiac, or else two half-zodiacs phased 6 months and 180 degrees apart (table 4).

Table 4

Stanza	Month	Sign(s)	
1	March	Aries	Corona (Libra)
2	April	(Taurus) Pleiades	
3	May	Gemini	Jupiter (Sagittarius)
4	June	Cancer	Cygnus (Capricorn)
5	July	(Leo) Corona setting	
6	August	Virgo	Pisces
7			
8	September	Libra	Aries
9	October	(Scorpio) Hercules	
10	November	(Sagittarius) Jupiter	Gemini

Passing over stanza 7 for the present, we find that stanza 8, linked substantively to stanza 1 by its complaint mode, again corresponds to Aries–Libra: the 'source of life' fits the first sign Aries, the lawyers' bowers the Scales of Justice. Stanza 9 refers mythologically to Hercules, a constellation with the same longitude as Scorpio. (The 'branch of honour' alludes to *Ramus pomifer*, an apple branch forming part of the constellation Hercules in visual portrayals.[49]) And stanza 10 is explicitly the place of 'the Twins', Gemini, though the mention of 'Jove' also indicates, as in stanza 3, Jupiter's domicile Sagittarius. Stanzas 8–10 could thus be regarded as beginning a new zodiacal garland, and as corresponding to stanzas 1–3. This hypothesis receives confirmation from the forms of the variable refrain: stanzas 1 and 8, 2 and 9 'the bridal day'; 3 and 10 'their bridal day'.[50]

We may deal here with another refrain variation, the use of 'upon' instead of 'against' in stanzas 6 and 9. On the first occasion the words belong to the rehearsal of the song 'prepared . . . against their

[47] Ptolemy put Cygnus in Capricornus $4°$–Aquarius $14°$ (Boll 106).
[48] Originating in Venus' and Cupid's metamorphoses into fish to escape Typhoeus: Ovid *Met.* 5.331; C. Middleton *The history of heaven* (1596) sigs. D 3v–4r. [49] Allen 242 cites the 1488 Hyginus.
[50] As against sts 4, 5 'their bridal day', 6 'your bridal day', 7 'their wedding day'. On numerological refrain variations in other Elizabethan poems see Hieatt *Short Time's Endless Monument* 10, Fowler *Triumphal Forms* 72, 100, 158, 160–1.

bridal day', so that the variation suitably anticipates the actual arrival of the day *upon* which it will formally be sung. The implication is that 'upon' in stanza 9 should similarly mark, somehow, the bridal day itself. And so it does. Stanza 9 corresponds in the astronomical scheme to Scorpio, the wedding sign.[51] Since the wedding was on 8 November, that is before Sol entered Sagittarius, the final stanza could not correspond both to the wedding month (November: Sagittarius) and to the wedding sign (Scorpio: 14 October–13 November). Spenser plays down this snag by giving prominence to the opposite sign and to 'the Twins of Jove'. But he also takes advantage of the associations of Sagittarius and November, to widen the poem's scope. On 17 November came an occasion of great importance, the Accession Day Feast commemorating what Queen Elizabeth was fond of calling her marriage to England. Spenser can therefore choose to look forward to the Queen's and the nation's future prospect, as well as the brides'. When he describes the bridegrooms as 'Beseeming well the bower of any queen' he echoes 'Fit to deck maidens' bowers' and implies that Elizabeth too is a bride.[52] (It is pleasant to note that one of her bowers decked with flowers of chivalry was Greenwich, famous for its stellar ornament—'tanquam sidereae domus cathedra'.[53]) Spenser thus sets the alliance solemnized in the betrothal within a context of larger, national associations.

The Anomalous Stanza.

It may be objected that stanza 7 breaks the zodiacal sequence. However, this apparent exception turns out to prove the rule most elegantly, for the same stanza is anomalous formally. Its refrain— 'Against their wedding day, which was not long'—constitutes the only departure from 'bridal day'. Moreover, its stanza form is also anomalous metrically. The other stanzas, some with a scheme of 6

---

[51] The uncertain betrothal date makes farther construction perilous. But if Norton is right in dating the betrothal 7–29 Sept. (*Background* 85), the spousal sign may well have been Virgo, so that the refrain variant 'upon' in st.6 would have a similar function to that in st.9.

[52] A point developed in Woodward 35 and Norton 'Queen Elizabeth's "Bridal Day" '. On Elizabeth's own use of the idea, see J.B.Black *The Reign of Elizabeth* (Oxford 1959) 19; on the idea itself, Robertson *Preface to Chaucer* 375.

[53] On stellification consult I.E.Rathborne *The Meaning of Spenser's Fairyland* (New York 1937). For Leland's eulogy of Greenwich see *Cygnea cantio* sig. C 3.

rhymes, others with 7, are grouped in 3 sets of 3, perhaps corresponding to the 3 signs of the spring, summer and autumn seasons. But
stanza 7 is unique in having only 5 rhymes (table 5). We can only conclude that the much-emphasized anomaly is intentional: that it
constitutes one of those sophistications of expected schemes, in which
mannerist artists delighted.[54]

Table 5

Stanza	Rhyme scheme	No. of rhymes
1–3	a b b a a b c b c c d d e d e e f f	6
4–6	a b b a a c d c d d e e f e f f g g	7
7	a b b a a b c b c c d d e d e e b b	5
8–10	a b b a a c d c d d e e f e f f g g	7

The introduction of Echo in stanza 7 suggests that it may be regarded as a digression, which instead of advancing the zodiac merely
repeats its predecessor's signs. The rhyme-pattern supports this view,
in that the rhymes *abound–confound–rebound* and *long–song* from stanza
6 are immediately taken up in 7, the only stanza to use the refrain
rhyme internally:

> So ended she; and all the rest around
> To her redoubled that her undersong,
> Which said, their bridal day should not be long.
> And gentle Echo from the neighbour ground,
> Their accents did resound.[55]

Moreover, there is an unmistakeable self-reference in the stanza's
account of how the Lee, lacking a tongue, 'did by signs his glad affection show,/ Making his stream run slow.' The hyperbole pays a
splendid compliment: by running slowly the river fondly delays the
brides' voyage downstream ('Adown the Lee') to Greenwich, in
double allusion to Orpheus' slowing of the Peneus and to the Tiber's
'flowing back with silent wave' to help Aeneas on his way to form an
alliance critical for New Troy.[56] But the lines may contain a formal

[54] J.Shearman *Mannerism* (Harmondsworth 1967) 140–51 *et passim*;
F. Würtenberger *Mannerism* tr. M.Heron (New York etc. 1963); Fowler
Triumphal Forms ch.5 and Index s.v. *Mannerism*.
[55] The rhyme link is noticed in F.L.Gwynn et al. *The Case for Poetry*
(Englewood Cliffs, N.J. 1954) 331.
[56] *Aen.* 8.86–9. Contrast Drayton's perfunctory handling of the motif:
'And let us sing so rare a verse,/ Our Beta's praises to rehearse,/ That little
birds shall silent be, to hear poor shepherds sing,/ And rivers backward
bend their course, and flow unto the spring' (*Shepherd's garland* 3.57–60, ed.
Hebel et al. 1.56.

subtlety: Spenser too can 'show' affection without words (that is, express numerologically) 'by signs' of the zodiac that change their pace.

The anomaly allows stanza 7 to be at once in and out of account formally, and so gives rise to a double symmetry. If it is left out, the stanzas number 9, in 3 groups of 3 by rhyme scheme. Then the crowning of the brides (stanza 5, the sovereign central digit of the 9) is in the place of honour at the poem's centre: 1, 2, 3 | 4, 5, 6 | 8, 9, 10. If, on the other hand, the anomalous stanza is included, a symmetry about its axis puts Cynthia at the sovereign centre, flanked by trios of stanzas with similar rhyme schemes: 4, 5, 6 | 7 | 8, 9, 10—a nice expression of the relativity of a bride's status on her wedding day.

Spenser may have had several reasons for wanting 9 stanzas. He wrote partly in emulation of Drayton's *Shepherd's garland,* whose eclogue-total avowedly symbolized the 9 Muses and implicitly matched a prominent image of his poem as of *Prothalamion,* Ariadne's nine-starred crown.[57] Again, Spenser would perhaps wish to proportion his two garlands. The half-zodiac of stanzas 8–10, like the 180 degrees mimed by the line-total, suggests from one point of view the incompleteness of betrothal, which is, as it were, only half a spousal. But *Prothalamion* is also a wedding song. If we remove the anomalous stanza (denoted by 7, a number of singularity and virginity), the proportion between the zodiac-garlands is 6 : 3 or 2 : 1, that is, the harmonious proportion of the octave conventional in epithalamium division.[58]

The Garlands Numbered.

If Spenser had reasons for the notional stanza total of 9, more compelling reasons determined the real stanza total of 10.

[57] *The shepherd's garland. Fashioned in nine eclogues. Rowland's sacrifice to the nine Muses.* Ariadne's crown is treated at 3.78 ff. On the constellation's description as 9 (occasionally 10) stars, see Allen 178. (A *locus classicus* is Ovid *Fasti* 3.515–16, where Bacchus changes the 9 jewels of Ariadne's crown into stars: 'dicta facit gemmasque novem transformat in ignes: / aurea per stellas nunc micat illa novem.') The count was familiar, appearing e.g. in C. Middleton's popular *History of heaven:* 'Then of nine silver stars is made a crown, / A garland beauty's goddess once did twine, / And gave to Ariadne for a boon' (sig. B 1).
[58] For 7 as virgin see Macrobius *In somn. Scip.* 1.6.10, ed. Stahl 102 and n.; for 7 *singularis et immobilis,* Valeriano cit. Fowler *Numbers of Time* 58 n.; for the octave proportion in epithalamia, Fowler *Triumphal Forms* 159–60.

Ovid's Flora wished to count the colours of her flowers, in vain.[59] But Spenser's flowers can be counted easily, since he specifies only 5 kinds: violet, daisy, lily, primrose, rose. This number, which receives farther emphasis from the presentation of the garlands in the fifth stanza, was chosen as a nuptial number. As such it played a part in ancient marriage ceremonies and their Renaissance poetic equivalents, and attracted a good deal of commentary. George Chapman explains that 5 was the number of torches at a wedding 'To show the union married loves should use,/Since in two equal parts it will not sever,/ But the midst holds one to rejoin it ever,/As common to both parts'— and because it united the first male and female numbers.[60] Jonson's wedding masque *Hymenaei* makes a similar point, to the accompaniment of arithmological annotation.[61] J. C. Scaliger's full account of the epithalamic genre follows Plutarch in suggesting various explanations for the 5 tapers, including symbolism of the 5 gods of marriage.[62] And Pietro Bongo adds Plato's limitation of wedding guests to 5 male and 5 female friends. Spenser carries this last programme out religiously, for he mentions just 10 individuals in *Prothalamion*, 5 female and 5 male.[63] The same consideration, together with the notion of a double spousal or twin 5's, seems to have determined the stanzaic organization: it consists, as we have seen, of 2 'garlands' each of 5 stanzas.[64]

Other numerical decorums abound. For instance, most of the floral imagery comes early, flowers being mentioned in exactly half the stanzas: $f, f, -, f, f \mid -, -, -, f, -$. The flower of stanza 9 is distinguished by its figurativeness and by referring to Essex instead of the 4 betrothed, so that a $(4+1)$ pattern results. The pattern recurs formally in the distribution of the flower stanzas, which are grouped $(4+1) \mid (1+4)$. The single flower stanza in the second garland links the groups

---

[59] *Fasti* 5.213–14: 'saepe ego digestos volui numerare colores/ nec potui.'
[60] *Hero and Leander* 5.324–7, ed. Bartlett 159. The whole passage leading up to Alcmane's and Mya's wedding (in the *fifth* Sestiad) is relevant; I am grateful to Mrs A. Mellor for drawing the connection to my notice.
[61] See Fowler *Triumphal Forms* 148–50.
[62] Iupiter, Venus, Diana, Iuno and Suada; see Scaliger 3.101; p.152A.
[63] Bongo 253; Plato *De legibus* 6.775. Spenser's guest list: the queen, 2 brides, 2 nymphs presenting crowns (female); 2 patrons, 2 bridegrooms, Spenser (male). 10 also numbered the months to full term: Statius *Silv.* 1.2.268; Jonson *Hymenaei* 546, ed. Herford and Simpson 7.228.
[64] On 5 as a common part-total in epithalamia, see Fowler *Triumphal Forms* 151.

together; just as Essex, the flower of chivalry, brings the 4 young people together at his house for their betrothal. A similar pattern governs refrain variations—a feature generally worth close attention.[65] In 5 stanzas the first refrain line ends with 'which is not long', in the other 5 with 'which was not long'. The distribution again forms the (4+1) motif: *is, was, was, was, was | is, was, is, is, is*. So too with the expression of personal feeling in stanzas 1 and 8, which Spenser himself describes (and critics have recently agreed with him) as plaintive intrusions: 'here fits not well/ Old woes'. Each half or stanza-garland thus comprises 4 festive and 1 plaintive stanzas; 4 stanzas of concord and calm, 1 of discord and care.[66]

A simpler decorum relates the content of some stanzas to their ordinal numbers. Thus 3 comparisons of whiteness come in stanza 3; sevenfold Echo, and the 7 planets whose music she symbolized,[67] in stanza 7; and a Muse in stanza 9.

Refrain and Complaint.

Such rudimentary if difficult enquiries, formal, schematic, iconological, must eventually be seen as preliminary to the more inward problems which interpreters are already quite properly immersed in. Consider the element of complaint. Daniel Woodward may be right in diagnosing a dark, ominous, psychologically disturbed (though surely not a 'poisonous') mood (p. 37; cf. 41). It would be easy for someone with Spenser's background—not least for a client of Essex's — to feel political bitterness. And the first stanza could no doubt be categorized as a client's complaint. But the 'old woe' expressed seems regret and trouble rather than bitterness: a melancholy sense, perhaps, of the fugacity of life and of patrons, prompted by the brilliant occasion next door to well-remembered Leicester House. Harry Berger (pp. 365-8) goes farther than Woodward, interiorizing the whole narrative of stanzas 2-7: he contrasts the past tense of vision with the 'present tense of utterance', the impulse to escape with the power of art (and the 'creative will') to endow revived memory with meaning. Psychological interpretation of the time structure in terms of 'lyric

[65] See n. 50 above.
[66] For 4 = stability and concord, the authority was Macrobius *In somn. Scip.* 1.6.22–33, ed. Stahl 104–6. See Fowler *Numbers of Time* 26–33.
[67] Conti 5.6, p. 454; cf. above ch. 3 n. 46. Drayton has a similar decorum in *Pastorals* (1619) 3.85–7, ed. Hebel et al. 2.530: 'day's most dearest light,/ With thy bright sister Cynthia, the glory of the night,/ And those that make ye seven' (in the 7th st.).

self-concern' may eventually be possible. But it is surely premature until simpler explanations of the tenses have been considered. Here the ceremonial pattern discussed in the last section is seen to have a decisive critical bearing. If the variation of tenses belongs to that pattern it probably refers to public rather than private concerns. Again, the use of the present tense in stanza 6 (the inset epithalamium prepared for the bridal day) suggests that in *Prothalamion* tense has less to do with imitation of the poet's consciousness than with imitation of the calendar and the brides' marital status. We find that the past-tense refrain variant correlates with the River Lee and the brides, the present-tense variant with the River Thames and London, where the bridegrooms wait (see table 6). The interweaving thus accords with the symbolic basis of all river spousals: the idea that confluent rivers unite indissolubly—'As meeting streams, both to our selves were lost;/ We were one mass'.[68] Just as the Lee changes its name when it joins the Thames, so do the brides change theirs at marriage.[69] (To draw attention to this matter of names as well as to pay suitable compliments, there are wordplays on *Somerset* and *Devereux* in stanzas 4 and 9, respectively.[70])

Table 6

Stanza	Refrain	Location
1	is	'Themmes'
2	was	'the flood thereby' (Lee)
3	was	'the Lee'
4	was	'the crystal flood' (Lee)
5	was	'the waves' (Lee)
6	is	—
7	was	'Adown the Lee'
8	is	'London'
9	is	'Essex House'
10	is	'river's side' (Thames)

But *Prothalamion*'s interweaving of past and present is by no means limited to *entrelacement* of betrothal and wedding, unmarried and

[68] Dryden *All for love* 3.95–6.
[69] A metamorphosis possibly assisted by the ambiguity in *Lee*, noticed Variorum *Minor Poems* 2.500. Though Lee primarily means River Lee, the sense 'Thames Bank' may operate secondarily, making the brides fallow (virgin) meadows garlanding the male river.
[70] i.e. the female and male squares. On the *summer's heat-Somerset* wordplay see J. N. Smith 176. Essex's name promises happiness (153–4) because *Devereux* will become (*devenir*) happy (*heureux*) (Grosart).

married estates. Besides marrying male and female (together with the related polarities of virginity and sexuality, Leda and Jupiter, lily and rose), this alliance of families conjoins polarities of a different order. First, it unites old and new social cadres. Worcester belonged to the older Catholic nobility, Petre and Guldeford to the newer gentry (their suitability for the queen's bower lies in 'gifts of wit and ornaments of nature' rather than in rank). Petre's having studied at the Middle Temple occasions another digressive contrast, between the proud 'templar knights' of a former age and the 'studious lawyers' of the emergent professionally trained administrative class. In these historical polarities of old and new, Spenser scrupulously excludes any undiscriminating value-preference. The Templar Knights 'decayed through pride', but were not always decayed; the generous Leicester's patronage gave place to comparative 'friendlessness', but also to the new patronage of Essex. No doubt Spenser had to adjust to difficult changes. But calling *Prothalamion*'s country passage an escapist flight from the reality of society's cares must be simplistic and wrong. On the one hand, the meadows around London really were idyllic by comparison with the city; on the other, the city could for Spenser be 'merry' (l. 128) as well as oppressive. Neither truth was more 'real': at its best the pastoral antithesis of town and country always eludes such a resolution.

The Refrain.

Berger offers the congenial suggestion that the brides move 'down the river of life and time', 'escaping the irreversible current even while opening themselves to the future' (p. 378). *Prothalamion*'s rivers are indeed ambivalent, for they combine implications of fertility, in the flowery meadows, with mutability, in their irreversible motion. The application is very general, as frequent imitations of the refrain have shown. Spenser's Thames follows the course of individual lives, but also of the national life—and of time itself. The unvarying 'Sweet Themmes run softly, till I end my song' acquires something of the force of destiny, like Catullus' epithalamic refrain of the Fates: 'currite ducentes subtegmina, currite, fusi'.[71]

In the light of the foregoing argument, something of the fullness of Spenser's great refrain can be appreciated. Primarily 'the bridal day, which is not long' refers to the time from the betrothal (perhaps

---

[71] *Carm.* 64, a paradigmatic epithalamium.

September) to the wedding (8 November). Secondarily it refers to the shortness of days as against nights in November, at the latitude of London. On a deeper level, however, the words express regret at the shortness of happiness in general: not only of the festive period of engagement, but of marriage and of mortal life (Berger 368, 377). Poets like swans sing before death, so that 'till I end my song' means 'until I complete my life's singing'. Spenser desires a quiet old age, and prays that his life may pass 'softly', not 'haste without stop to a devouring sea'.[72] But pathos is the least of the refrain's effects. It also implies the reflection that whether the 'brave Muse [who] may sing/ To ages following' of Elizabeth's name and Essex's exploits is himself or not, his poetry will in any case outlast them all. Here as elsewhere Spenser fronts posterity more confidently than any previous English poet. The refrain aspires to nothing less than the hope that *Prothalamion* will be coeval with Thames, with England itself. Indeed, more audaciously still, it takes its own existence as a guarantee of duration, adjuring the nation to be at peace, to run softly, until *Prothalamion* ends—which is never, since the song is a circular one and therefore endless. The call for peaceful accord was not superfluous: within four years Essex's life was to flow on an executioner's block.

Moral Panegyric.

Mannerist poets were often conscious of the political implications of their art; of their power to confer glory and confirm status.[73] And we might expect that on an important nuptial occasion a poet aware of court factions would be particularly careful to write what was socially acceptable. Spenser himself speaks of the alliances celebrated in *Prothalamion* as calling for protection against 'friendship's faulty guile' and against 'foes' who would be confounded by 'fruitful issue' (st. 6). The poem is in fact decorous, embracing and hierarchically ordering everyone—brides, bridegrooms, bridesmaids, queen, patron, poet— who on such an occasion should be raised to the heavens. No-one will enjoy it, who does not appreciate Spenser's entering into the event, his triumphant assimilation and conversion of fact into poetic form. Indeed, the form of the occasion, as we have seen, occasioned the form of *Prothalamion*. For a double betrothal, everything is paired: brides and bridegrooms, stanza-garlands and zodiacs, rivers (Thames

---

[72] Cowley *Bathing in the river* in *The mistress*, ed. Waller 151.
[73] See Würtenberger, esp. 36–9.

and Lee), patrons (Leicester and Essex), poets (Spenser and 'some brave Muse'), demigods (Cynthia–Elizabeth and Hesperus–Essex). There are even two poems, the narrative-mythological *Prothalamion* and the inset spousal of stanza 6 in a more lyric kind.[74]

But decorum need not mean uniform hyperbole. Several critics of *Prothalamion* have found in it the intricately-concealed admonitions of recommendatory panegyric. Woodward (pp. 38-41) detects moral complexities in the elaborately emphasized whiteness of the swans. And Berger (pp. 366-7) finds malaise, awkward hesitation, difficulty over decorum, and even 'logical inconsistency' in the same feature. It is true that the third stanza's elaborate *copulatio* on 'white' discriminates narrowly between sorts of innocence. A white swan symbolized purity, *candor* meaning moral as much as physical whiteness.[75] Woodward's theory of a 'violent contrast' between the swan's purity and the water's impurity might thus seem to have iconographical support. But his un-Elizabethan inference is that the swans who resemble angels are nevertheless 'products of human passion' ('Somersheat') and that 'fruitful love is not only a controlled outgrowth of lust, but also a natural one'. There is no need to explain the mention of chastity so elaborately. Betrothal was an occasion when the sanctity of the virgin-knot was rather apt to be remembered, sometimes with a warning—'Take heed/ As Hymen's lamps shall light you'.[76] But the topic would naturally be a more delicate one for Spenser than for the fictional Prospero; hence, perhaps, the veil of mythology. The swan incident occasioned by Leda's purity might signify (according to a standard interpretation of divine rapes) no more than the supernaturality of the union. It would be remarkable indeed if Spenser wrote anything to suggest that the brides' shrinking from the 'gentle stream', which 'seemed foul to them', was excessively prim. We have to allow for 'seemed foul to them' meaning 'seemed foul in comparison to them'. In all probability the waves shrink away (it is not they who draw back) simply as an auspicious omen: the swan was thought

---

[74] On kinds of epithalamium, see Scaliger 3.101; p.154. *Proth.* has the mixed narrative and lyrical form of Catullus *Carm.*64.
[75] See Valeriano ch.23 'Olor. Animi candor', cit. Tervarent s.v. *Cygne* 8 'La pureté de l'âme', cols.140–1.
[76] *Tempest* 4.1.13–23, inverting the imagery of *Proth.*: 'disdain and discord shall bestrew/ The union of your bed with weeds so loathly. . . . ' Chastity was a common topic of epithalamia: e.g. *Let mother earth* in *Old Arcadia* 3rd Eclogues, ed. Robertson 246.

lucky by sailors 'quia numquam mergitur undis'.[77] Images of white-ness could even be erotic as in Martial's 'loto candidior puella cygno, argento, nive, lilio, ligustro'.[78] Berger (pp. 371, 373) has diagnosed 'daunger' in the brides' reluctance, found Daphne metamorphosed in the Peneus, and seen the inset song as counselling against sex guilt ('love's dislike'). But Spenser's oblique recommendation is more nicely balanced: 'let your bed with pleasures *chaste* abound'. The des-cription of the swans no more implies that the brides were specially inhibited than that of the flowers did. There can be no doubt, how-ever, that the encomium advances ideals as much as compliments.

Spenser's praise of Essex is no less complex, although it has been taken as conventionally hyperbolic or 'patron-seeking'. Berger even speculates that Spenser may be giving a sample of professional journey-work, 'what a paid poet *might* sing' (p. 375); which is surely to make him sophisticated in an impossibly modern way. There is no evidence that Spenser wrote *Prothalamion* to attract patronage. More probably, in view of the time its composition must have required, it was commissioned by Essex or Worcester.

If *Prothalamion* is a poem of patronage, it succeeds in being remark-ably free from unqualified panegyric. Take the gratuitous remark that the Templar Knights 'decayed through pride'. What possible rele-vance or function can this have, but a moral one? So that when we

---

[77] Servius *In Aen.* 1.393; cf. Isidore *Origines* 12.7, 19. Spenser's collocation of swans with Zephyrus might be associated with specific emblems; but again ambiguities swarm—HONOR ALIT ARTES and gratitude for patronage, but also SIBI CANIT ET ORBI and resignation to age. See A. Henkel and A. Schöne *Emblemata* (Stuttgart 1967) col. 815, Costalius' CYCNUS. HONOR ALIT ARTES, 'Non canit assueta Cycnus vocalis in unda,/ Ni Zephyri spiret mollior aura sibi. . . ./Sic tua Mecoenas circunstetit auro Maronem', and col. 816, Camerarius' ASPIRET MOLLIOR AURA and SIBI CANIT ET ORBI, 'Ipsa suam celebrat sibi mens bene conscia mortem,/ Ut solet herbiferum Cygnus ad Eridanum.' In Leland the motif is meant in the former sense: 'Sed neque Cygni canunt, nisi flante zephyro, vento geniali quidem illo, si quicquam Aeliani Graeci iudicio tribuendum . . .' (Introd., sig. A 4v). With *Proth.* sts 1, 3, cf. Leland B 1r 'Et spirat Zephyrus, novumque pictos/ Ver fundit vario colore flores./ Cygnus me peperit nive, et colostro/ Mater candidior'.

[78] *Epig.* 1.115.23 'a girl desires me, whiter than a washed swan, than silver, snow, lily, privet'; cf. Ovid *Met.* 13.789, 796. But Reusner's swan emblem reapplies Martial's words to *virtuous* whiteness: 'Albo candidius quid est olore,/ Argento, nive, lilio, ligustro/ Fides candida, candidique mores . . .' (Henkel and Schöne col. 814).

come to 'those high towers' next door to the Temple, and hear how Essex

> Like radiant Hesper when his golden hair
> In th'Ocean billows he hath bathed fair,
> Descended to the river's open viewing,

we may find moral recommendation in this too. The lines imply not only a god's descent, but also a man's condescension from the high towers of dignity.[79] Panegyric here contains a suggestion as salutary, and possibly as unpalatable, as any in the cautionary letter which Bacon wrote to Essex in the same year:[80] namely, that he should stoop more from the height of ambitious greatness and merge his own in his country's life (symbolized by the Thames). The admonition is at once gravest and most covert in its allusion to Virgil's Pallas, who when he had bathed in Ocean's billows resembled the morning star, 'qualis ubi Oceani perfusus Lucifer unda'.[81] Of course the change to Hesperus 'love's harbinger'[82] (sanctioned by the close association of morning and evening stars) suits the present occasion.[83] But the replacement of *Lucifer* makes a point which is judiciously, rather than blandly, encomiastic. It is not allowed, however, to detract from the main impression of Essex in the splendid role of Hesper, whom the poets invoked in epithalamia (as Scaliger notes[84]) because his appearance was anciently the sign to light nuptial torches. As 'the amorous evening star',[85] Essex greets the brides and signals the completion of the bridal day.

Old Woes.

Discussions of *Prothalamion* have usually dwelt on the jarring tone of complaint. This is certainly unusual in spousal poems—as indeed the poet's pretended recollection of the paradigm acknowledges (l. 141).

[79] High towers could mean proud loftiness, on the basis of *Is.* 2.15, 30.25.
[80] See Black 424. For a more sanguine view of Essex as 'protector of the state' see Woodward 42–4.
[81] *Aen.* 8.589. cf. Ovid *Ex ponto* 2.5.49–50 'surgit Iuleo iuvenis cognomine dignus,/ qualis ab Eois Lucifer ortus aquis'; Homer *Il.* 5.1–6; Seneca *Hipp.* 749–52; Tasso *Gerus. lib.* 15.60, *Rinaldo* 5.14.
[82] Milton's phrase: *Par. Lost* 11.589.
[83] On identification of Hesper and Lucifer see Cartari 285. For ambivalence of the morning star cf. *F.Q.* 1.12.21, 2.12.65, 6.7.19. Contrast Sidney's treatment of the identity, 51 above.
[84] 3.101, p. 152A; cr. Jonson *Hymenaei* 356n., ed. Herford and Simpson 7.222.
[85] Donne *Lincoln's Inn epithalamium* 61.

Nor can we quite treat the two plaintive stanzas as digressions. Although only stanzas 1 and 8 are formally plaintive, suggestions of mutability recur, to give the refrain sad overtones, and almost to make the flowers emblems of human frailty. We cannot but recall that the same Peneus where Ariadne was married also witnessed Aristaeus asking 'Why was I born, to be hated of the Fates?'[86] However, Berger is right to describe Spenser's complaint as resolved through the distancing process of poetic mediation and 'the inward mastery of experience' (p. 376). *Prothalamion* undoubtedly gives an impression of emotional resolution. In part, perhaps, it achieves this through its metamorphoses: snow to river, green-haired nymphs to nymphs with floral crowns, swans to brides, mortals to stars. Its mythology expresses a sense of natural process, rather than merely the semi-divine (aristocratic) status of the participants. In this way *Prothalamion* establishes the larger context necessary to philosophical consolation. Moreover, like Chaucer's *Book of the duchess* it resolves complaint into formal order—the order, here, of a highly structured cosmic image. Eventually, it achieves generic transmutation, so that the plaintive gives place to the festive, woe to joy.

I have tried to show how the continuity of *Prothalamion* depends on its occasion. However, it would be wrong to attribute the poetic unity to an occasion that after all could have given rise to other very different poems. *Prothalamion*'s unity has more to do with the thought that combines its thematic sequences, its *paysage moralisé* of familial rivers, its vegetative imagery (seed, branch, flowers, floral crowns), its ordered constellations of stellified celebrants, its interconnected myths of Jupiter, Leda and others, and its moral statements about virginity and marriage. All these elements contribute to a meditation on changed estate and the generation of new forms. Growth and renewal; the balance of old and new in national and individual life; time's giving and taking: these are ultimately what *Prothalamion* is about. If the poet's persona is a disappointed suitor, the poet himself is oppressed by something more: the vanity of appearance's 'empty shadows' (l.9). In his search for reality he repeatedly pursues the origins of being: the physical origin of the Peneus in Mount Pindus;[87] the mythological origin of the Twins in Jupiter's amour with Leda;

---

[86] Virgil *Georg.* 4.315 ff.

[87] See Ovid *Met.* 1.452–569, 12.209; Strabo 9.3.12; Pliny *Hist. nat.* 4.8.15.31; Livy 32.15; Hyginus *Fab.* 203; Parthenius *Erotica* 15; Pausanius 8.20.2, 10.5.3; Pomponius Mela 2.3; Diodorus Siculus 4; Aelian *Var hist.* 3.1.

the debatable origin of the swans ('angels' breed' or 'bred of Summer's heat'); the historical origin of the Inns of Court; and his own personal origins in London, 'this life's first native source', and in 'an house of ancient fame'. A similar preoccupation appears in a sustained insistence on the meaning and the changing of names—river names, Somerset, the 'glorious name' of Eliza and the 'dreadful name' of Essex—not to speak of the ancient source of his own.

Prothalamion thus approaches similar problems of reality and phenomenality to those of Heraclitus' famous river-statement. Indeed, it may be thought to echo Seneca's version of the Heraclitean fragment: 'we descend, and yet do not descend, into the same river twice. (For the name or identity of the river is the same, but its water changed.)'[88] Since Essex as Hesper already 'hath bathed' when he descends 'to the river's open viewing', he may *almost* be said to descend twice. As Professor Kirk (p. 377) has shown, Heraclitus' river-statement illustrates the coincidence between stability and change in such opposites as summer–winter and youth–age—similar *coincidentia* to those explored in *Prothalamion*. Even Spenser's structural use of fives has a relevance to this philosophical context, for Plutarch's discussion of the pentad connects it with the same Heraclitean principle of stability in change:

> As Heraclitus says that the principle which orders the whole by gradually changing makes the world out of itself and again itself out of the world . . . so the conjuction of the number five with itself by its nature generates nothing incomplete or of different character, but has changes which are determined.[89]

It would be idle to pretend that all the problems raised above are resolved or even capable of resolution. But discussing them will surely have shown that *Prothalamion* suffers far less from decorative vapidity than from a tendency to be overfreighted with close-packed content. If it has a certain abstract quality—'less an orange than a grid'[90]—it is nonetheless deeply rooted in the soil of its historical origins. As with many occasional poems, in fact, its difficulty is attributable less to remoteness from the natural world than to immersion in its

---

[88] 'In idem flumen bis descendimus et non descendimus. (Manet enim idem fluminis nomen, aqua transmissa est.)': Seneca *Epist.* 58.23. See G. S. Kirk *Heraclitus* (Cambridge 1954) 367 ff., esp. 373.
[89] *De E* 388 D–E; Kirk 345. Plutarch refers to the circular property of 5 whereby its powers end with the digit 5.
[90] D. Davie *Collected Poems 1950–1970* (1972) 10.

destructive element. The problem for the interpreter (as the foregoing, I fear, may have illustrated) is to know how much of the resuscitated occasion — how much soil about the roots — to include in his synthesis. A purely critical account might afford more tact in selection; but it would falsify the proportion of the event. We may have to face a cruel paradox, that the monumental ideal made for expendability: for a form uniquely suitable to a single unrepeatable occasion.

5

The Shakespearean Conceit

Future historians of criticism may well be struck by how much more interest our age has shown in Metaphysical imagery than in Elizabethan. The different rates of scholarly publication in the two fields will certainly provide them with some remarkable contrasts.[1] Statistics hardly seem necessary, if one thinks how hard it would be to find books on Elizabethan poetry comparable with those of Williamson, Warnke, Summers, Miner, Stein, Alvarez, Miller, Richmond and Fish, to name only a few. There are, of course, many works on individual Elizabethan writers; but almost none that treat their style in general, unless as a preliminary to Metaphysical style. No doubt our successors may see the preference as manifesting some movement of taste, even of thought, which it would be ridiculous to think of escaping, if we ever became aware of it. But they will possibly also wonder why we took so long to remove obstacles well within our lesser reach, which hamper appreciation of Elizabethan imagery need-lessly.

Metaphysical and Spenserian Conceits.

In 1946 Rosemond Tuve detected 'a growing tendency to forsake Elizabethan for Jacobean poets'.[2] Since then neglect of the Eliza-bethans has become almost total, interrupted only by a partial re-covery of Spenser and by some diachronic forays tracing motifs or intellectual traditions. Shakespeare is the great exception: his *Sonnets* have not lost favour.[3] They have been lumped awkwardly with Meta-

---

[1] e.g. the bibliography in K. K. Ruthven *The Conceit* (1969) 61–4, which lists twice as many studies in the later period.

[2] *Elizabethan and Metaphysical Imagery* (Chicago 1947) 6.

[3] Generic descriptions include L. C. John *The Elizabethan Sonnet Sequences: Studies in Conventional Conceits* (New York 1938) and K. K. Ruthven 'The Poet as Etymologist' *CQ* 11 (1969) 9–37. Shakespeare is only partly an exception: J. M. Nosworthy, e.g., finds 'altogether too much of the working out of conceits': see *Shakespeare* ed. S. Wells (1973) 48.

physical poetry, however; and interpreters have found great difficulties in them, not all due to the privacy of their social context. Rosemond Tuve was surely right in arguing that we misconstrue the rhetorical functions of Renaissance imagery. But that hardly explains why a barrier obstinately separates Tudor and Stuart poetry, with only Shakespeare by his genius obscurely breaking it. The powerful demonstrations of *Elizabethan and Metaphysical Imagery* mostly go to bring the two periods of literature together, rather than to distinguish between them in any way that could explain or counteract an unreasonable preference for one. It is much the same with J. A. Mazzeo's connection of seventeenth-century imagery with a poetic of universal analogy.[4] We may agree with his critique of attempts to explain the Metaphysical style in terms of Petrarchism, the emblem tradition, Ramistic logic, or the Baroque.[5] And we may accept, with reservations, his theory that the Metaphysical poets 'possessed a view of the world founded on universal analogy and derived habits of thought which prepared them for finding and easily accepting the most heterogeneous analogies.'[6] (T. E. May's point—that *correspondencia* in Gracián is not a metaphysical concept—may be thought a local objection, hardly impairing the general theory.) Few will doubt that cosmic analogies, both familiar and occult, played a great part in Metaphysical poetry, even if no-one can reasonably believe that every conceit enshrined a serious philosophical correspondence. However, Professor Mazzeo's theory applies to the sixteenth century no less than to the seventeenth. Giordano Bruno, with whom the practice and theory of the heuristic use of analogy coincide, comes in the earlier period.[7] And on the other hand the English Reformers increasingly challenged the doctrine of *analogia entis*, from the late sixteenth century onwards. Mazzeo might have used his Hegel *symbolon* ('When philosophy paints its gray in gray, a shape of life has grown old') more narrowly, to imply that much seicento theory was retrospective, based on cinquecento practice. At any rate, we are left with

---

[4] *Renaissance and Seventeenth-Century Studies* (1964) chs. 1, 2; also 'A Critique of Some Modern Theories of Metaphysical Poetry' in *Seventeenth-Century English Poetry* ed. W. R. Keast (New York 1962) 63–74.
[5] Keast 65–9. [6] ibid. 73
[7] See ibid. 63–4; F. A. Yates 'The Emblematic Conceit in Giordano Bruno's *De gli eroici furori* and in the Elizabethan Sonnet Sequences' *JWI* 6 (1943) 101–21 and *Giordano Bruno and the Hermetic Tradition* (1964); and L. S. Lerner and E. A. Gosselin 'Giordano Bruno' *Sci. Amer.* 228 (April 1973) 86–94.

the question why Elizabethan conceits should be less accessible than Metaphysical ones. The habit of cosmic analogy, however applicable, was common to both periods. True, later analogies were often pressed farther; but that need not have made them more attractive.

We begin to wonder how far the distaste for Elizabethan imagery rests on informed value preferences, and whether some of the inaccessibility may not be self-created. Have critics possibly made their approach with an inappropriate mental set? At least they seem to have had an expectation that they would find Elizabethan conceits to be comparatively simple. Occasionally this is given a rationale in terms of contemporary theory: 'The relation between the object and its representation was relatively clear in the criticism of the cinquecento. For our [seicento] theorists the relationship was more complex.'[8] When in fact a critic finds late Elizabethan conceits intricate and oblique, he is liable to call them 'diffuse, vague, atmospheric' and 'shadowy'—the terms F. T. Prince applies to *Amoretti*.[9] Alternatively, he may deny that there is much in them besides their vehicles; as when Allen Tate writes of Spenser's 'ornamental decoration of image'; or when Jean Hagstrum thinks that 'the iconic poetry of Drayton . . . contents the eye' only.[10] In the same way, Austin Warren contrasts Spenser and Donne: the former's epic simile 'is fully pictorial; the intent . . . is decorative. On the other hand, the 'sunken' and the 'radical' types of imagery—the conceits of Donne . . . expect scant visualization.'[11] But visualization is far too limited a notion to be helpful with late Elizabethan imagery.[12] And a reader of dark conceits is unlikely to find the lights hidden beneath their surfaces, if he believes that plain superficiality bounds them.

Concentrate on the sensuous particulars of the vehicle in *Amoretti* 6, for example, and you might condemn such a phrase as 'gentle breast' for its stock epithet, or the whole sonnet for imprecision:

---

[8] Mazzeo *Studies* 43.

[9] 'The Sonnet from Wyatt to Shakespeare' *Elizabethan Poetry* ed. J. R. Brown and B. Harris (1960) 18–19.

[10] Tate *Reactionary Essays* (New York 1936) 74 cit. Tuve *Metaphysical Imagery* 216 n.; J. H. Hagstrum *The Sister Arts* (Chicago and London 1958) 100. On the indispensable terms *vehicle* and *tenor*, taken from I. A. Richards, see D. M. Miller *The Net of Hephaestus* (The Hague and Paris 1971) 42.

[11] E. A. Warren *Richard Crashaw: A study in Baroque Sensibility* (Baton Rouge, La 1939) 177 discussed Mazzeo 'A Critique', Keast 70.

[12] Mazzeo (ibid.) rightly deprecates stress on visualization; as does Tuve *Metaphysical Imagery* ch. 5 'The Criterion of Sensuous Vividness'.

The dureful oak, whose sap is not yet dried,
  Is long ere it conceive the kindling fire:
  But when it once doth burn, it doth divide
  Great heat, and makes his flames to heaven aspire.
So hard it is to kindle new desire,
  In gentle breast that shall endure for ever:[13]

But trace the correspondences of tenor and vehicle, and you find their members performing fairly complex functions. Thus, the vehicular oak, which holds out against attempts to ignite it but then burns greatly with lasting flames, resembles the virtuous lady, in that she resists easy lusts but may at last love devotedly and faithfully. The comparison selects meanings of *gentle* and modulates them to convey a particular excellence of courteous generosity which will not change troth once plighted.[14] Any contrariety between 'dureful' and 'gentle' is muted by the emblematic associations of the oak as *fortitudo* or moral virtue,[15] and by the common application of *gentle* to domestic varieties of trees.[16] When, however, we try to trace out the rest of the tenor and vehicle chains—a project that would be easy enough with a Metaphysical conceit—the difficulties of embedded, doubled and inverted metaphors are encountered. 'Divide / Great heat' unquestionably implies some such tenor as 'share great love'; a comparison depending on the conventional fire of love.[17] But one can hardly keep 'divide' (or, in another way, 'dureful') out of the abruptly changed metaphor that follows:

Deep is the wound, that dints the parts entire
With chaste affects, that naught but death can sever.

The wound of deep love paradoxically joins together and makes one flesh ('entire'; 'knits the knot'), so that oak-splitting turns out not to be a preliminary to burning. The resistant firmness of the tree's knotted grain, revalued in retrospect, is now seen to be insisted on by the extraordinarily-sustained *traductio* 'nought . . . not . . . not

---

[13] Variorum text: orthography modernized but not punctuation.
[14] See *OED* s.v. Gentle A 1 'noble', A 1 d 'excellent', A 3 'generous, courteous'. [15] See Tervarent s.v. *Chêne*, col.91.
[16] *OED* s.v. *Gentle* A 4 cites Holland (1601): 'the gentle garden cornel tree', Shakespeare *W. T.* 4.4.93 'We marry / A gentler scion to the wildest stock'.
[17] Possibly punning *divide* = 'share' (*OED* 8 b) and = 'give out in all directions' (*OED* 8 c, but with no earlier ex.). Several other puns in the sonnet are discussed in W. C. Johnson 'Spenser's *Amoretti* 6' *Explicator* 29.5 (1971) no. 38.

... naught ... not ... knot'. In this way the almost-unsplittable slow-burning fierce-burning divided-undivided oak corresponds to multiple tenors, distinct though not incompatible. Through these rhetorical labyrinths we are guided by traditional figurative applications, such as the proverbs 'heart of oak' and 'one stroke fells not an oak',[18] conveying the moral soundness of the lady and the magnitude of the work of courtship. Or consider 'makes his flames to heaven aspire'. The flames rise just as the love aspires to a heaven beyond its mortal reach, perhaps beyond it altogether. But take *aspire* to carry the implication 'die',[19] and the breast if not the love may reach heaven to endure indeed for ever. The entirely wounded tree and the funerary but amorous fire interrelate in a way that eludes logic.[20] Yet the effect is far from imprecise: these flames positively crackle with intelligence of passion.

G. K. Hunter's interesting account of *Amoretti* partly rests on prescriptive assumptions about what 'the English sonnet form, with its epigrammatic structure' ought to be, as it moves to 'final denouement', preferably in a couplet.[21] Like J. W. Lever, he blames Spenser for the generic error of attempting in sonnets what can only be accomplished in long poems; unjustly, since Elizabethan 'sonnet sequences' sometimes were long poems in quatorzain stanzas, with ample room for unresolved suspensions and prolonged meditation.[22] Neverthe-

---

[18] Tilley H 309 e.g. 'my heart is as sound as a bell, heart of oak' (1605), and T 496 e.g. 'It is but a simple oak, that [is] cut down at the first stroke' (1477) and 'It is not one stroke that can fell an oak' (1631). Submerged idioms like these often make local intention uncertain: cf. Miller 58, 80, 86.
[19] *OED* s.v. *Aspire* 5 'mount up'; also *ad fin.*, = *Expire*, e.g. Hellowes (1574): 'Christ aspiring upon the cross'; cf. Jonson *Poetaster* 1.1.83-4: 'Then, when this body falls in funeral fire, / My name shall live, and my best part aspire'.
[20] See Tervarent col. 184, s.v. *Flamme* 5, a funerary motif expressing death's finality. On the fire of love see Praz, Index s.v. *Fire; Flame; Cupid (Love) as stoker; Cupid blows the coals.*
[21] 'Spenser's *Amoretti* and the English Sonnet Tradition' in *A Theatre for Spenserians* ed. J. M. Kennedy and J. A. Reither (Toronto and Buffalo 1973) 134, 139; cf. 142-3. L. L. Martz has fortunately felt the need to defend Spenser's sonnets against the objection that they lack 'wit and compression': the brilliant result is 'The *Amoretti*: "Most Goodly Temperature" ', *Form and Convention* ed. Nelson 146-68.
[22] *A Theatre* 142-3; cf. Lever 102-3: 'Why then did Spenser confound two distinct ways of writing?' For reasons why sonnets should be regarded as stanzas, see A. Dunlop 'Calendar Symbolism in the "Amoretti" ' *N & Q* 214 (1969) 24-6 and 'The Unity of Spenser's *Amoretti*' in *Silent Poetry* 153-69; T. P. Roche in *English Poetry and Prose, 1540-1674* ed. C. Ricks (1970) 101-18;

less, Professor Hunter's perceptive descriptions of Spenser's 'characteristically self-involuted' syntax (p.135) deserve close attention. The observation that 'the effortless flow of analogies . . . often involves a genuine ambiguity between tenor and vehicle, between the point of comparison and the thing compared' (p.138) applies with equal force to *The Faerie Queen* and to many *Amoretti* stanzas. Instead of at once deploring this feature, however, we may wish to defer judgement a little.

Spenser's Complex Conceit.

Amoretti 1, which Hunter thinks deficient in argument, calls for rather extended treatment, as a fine but not uncharacteristic example of the neo-Petrarchan manner Spenser shared with Sidney and Shakespeare. As we should expect with a poem in such a well-developed tradition, the means to its passionate sensuousness are not simple, even if its effect seems so:

> Happy ye leaves when as those lily hands,
>> Which hold my life in their dead doing might
>> Shall handle you and hold in love's soft bands,
>> Like captives trembling at the victor's sight.
> And happy lines, on which with starry light,
>> Those lamping eyes will deign sometimes to look
>> And read the sorrows of my dying spright,
>> Written with tears in heart's close bleeding book.
> And happy rhymes bathed in the sacred brook,
>> Of Helicon whence she derived is,
>> When ye behold that angel's blessed look,
>> My soul's long lacked food, my heaven's bliss.
> Leaves, lines, and rhymes, seek her to please alone,
>> Whom if ye please, I care for other none.

The opening quatrain compares the white vibrating leaves of *Amoretti* held in the lady's hands to captives white and trembling before a triumphator who may take their lives. Ordinary captives' hard bonds, in the vehicle, correspond in the tenor to the soft fingers holding the book (and perhaps secondarily, if the book is bound, to

---

W. C. Johnson 'Rhyme and Repetition in Spenser's *Amoretti*' *Xavier Univ. Studies* 9 (1970) 15–25; Fowler *Triumphal Forms* ch.9. Subjects and themes continued through several sonnets have often been noticed in the 'sequences' of Spenser, Sidney and Shakespeare.

the cords binding its quires).[23] But since the lady's hands are those 'which hold my life in their dead doing might', the simile functions as a complex metaphor,[24] in whose embedded comparison it is the lover, conquered in an *amorosa guerrera*, who pretends to dread his mistress' mood. Thus, vibrating leaves held in fingers resemble captives held in physical bonds and trembling with fear, who in turn resemble the poet trembling with emotions of love, whether at the thought of Elizabeth's touch or of his life being figuratively in her hands:

vibrating leaves		trembling captives		trembling poet
tenor 1	*resembling*	*vehicle 1*		
		tenor 2	*resembling*	*vehicle 2*

Moreover, since poet and book belong to the same field of discourse, the complex metaphor is of a very special form, in which the more distant vehicle returns to the proximate literal chain. So far we can be reasonably sure of having constructed the conceit correctly— except possibly for some uncertainty as to whether tenor and vehicle may not be inverted, the sonnet being more about the lover than the book. But even at this stage of reading we have depended on the positiveness or congruence of the comparisons, which rest on the love-triumph tradition familiar from such works as Ovid's *Amores*, Petrarch's *Trionfi* and Colonna's *Hypnerotomachia*, and returned to in sonnets 29 and 52 of the present sequence.[25] If the metaphor submerged in 'love's soft bands' had been more novel or difficult in

[23] *OED* s.v. *Band* sb. I 1 fetter; I 2 loose tie, e.g. Shakespeare *Ven. and Adon.* st. 38 'Her arms infold him like a band'; I 2 b, the cords crossing the back of a book (no ex. before 1759; but cf. *Bind* v. III 11, common from ca 1400).
[24] I use *compound metaphor* in the sense defined in G.N. Leech *A Linguistic Guide to English Poetry* (1969) 159–61 ('the overlapping of two or more individual metaphors) but distinguish *complex* (embedded) metaphors and *double* or multiple metaphors with more than one vehicle or tenor. Contrast *compound* in Miller 131. Leech's account is useful; though adequate description would have to deal with grammatic and semantic aspects of chains of discourse, considered literally and metaphorically.
[25] See Fowler *Triumphal Forms* 38–61. Superstructural effects allowed by congruent comparison offset the arguments against congruence of C. Brooks and W.K. Wimsatt (e.g., that reliance on positive metaphor leads to *cliché*). See Miller 96–7 and 106; also 123, arguing that Neocritical criteria inevitably favoured Metaphysical poetry. Advantages of positive metaphor include a larger creative role for the reader (ibid. 133) and (I would add) greater communicative possibilities.

itself, it would have lessened the possibility of farther, superstructural effects.

Taking the metaphor of 'lily hands' into account brings us to stranger ground. Lilies hold leaves too, so that there is almost some thought of a double vehicle. At least, trembling of the lilies' leaves is suggested, and with it an idea that Elizabeth's hands may shake a little (like her proud heart in *Amoretti* 10) with the emotion the printed leaves are designed to arouse. The leaves will be happy, obviously, according to the poetic convention whereby a lover regards the 'experience' of objects enjoying physical contact with his mistress as enviable.[26] Less obviously, they will be fortunate when the trembling they engender indicates the successful effect of the poet's courtship. Ambiguity here expresses a reciprocity of relation that distinguishes *Amoretti* from most sonnet sequences: when Elizabeth is 'pleased' by the leaves (a stage very different from that of Sonnet 48, where she burns a confession of the poet's love), he as much as she will be 'victor'.[27]

To call the metaphoric structure circular or involuted would not do justice to its robust though gentle movement. Succeeding conceits of *Amoretti* 1 become more abstract as they rise towards the world of Ideas. One sequence of discourse runs through aspects of the book: the material 'leaves'; the communication of 'lines' looked on and 'sorrows' read; the poetic form, 'rhymes', drawn from higher vision. And corresponding aspects of the beloved ascend from 'hands', through 'eyes', to the 'angel's look' in them—that is, from physical through animate to spiritual levels. Each quatrain has an inset figure whose vehicle anticipates the next level. 'Victor's sight' looks on to 'lamping eyes' and optical activity in the second quatrain; copious tears and blood flow towards the 'sacred brook' of the third. Finally, 'bliss' makes the end of the *askesis* of souls (vegetable, animal, rational), just as it is the final cause of literary composition. The concluding summation can hardly be said to lack foundation in poetic logic.[28] The couplet asserts Spenser's seriousness, even his preference for instrumental values, at the same time as it refers, like *Astrophil and Stella* 1, after the manner of mannerism, to its own form. One could divide many narrow questions about ambiguities in this complicated

[26] See Ruthven *The Conceit* 20–2.
[27] Martz 152 ff. finds the relationship characterized by a rare mutuality of affection. *Amoretti* 17 uses the ambiguous application of *trembling* again.
[28] On the summation schema see Curtius 289–90.

sonnet. For the present purpose, we need only note the frequent switches from tenor to vehicle chains. A few words (*hold, trembled*) belong to both; but lexical as distinct from syntactical ambiguities are not specially noticeable.

Amoretti 15 seems at first to have a much simpler figurative structure. Consisting of a catalogue or blazon of features, visually compared each to some precious material, it might have been written to confirm Raymond Southall's thesis about commercial materialism in Elizabethan love poetry. Indeed, he discusses it as such: Spenser is like an enthusiastic salesman, and the sonnet 'flatters the lady by treating her as a precious but as yet unexploited commodity'.[29] But this appearance is deceptive. Spenser in fact criticizes the vain efforts of the 'tradeful merchants':

> Ye tradeful merchants, that with weary toil,
>> Do seek most precious things to make your gain;
>> And both the Indias of their treasures spoil,
>> What needeth you to seek so far in vain?
> For lo my love doth in her self contain
>> All this world's riches that may far be found,
>> If sapphires, lo her eyes be sapphires plain,
>> If rubies, lo her lips be rubies sound:
> If pearls, her teeth be pearls both pure and round;
>> If ivory, her forehead ivory ween;
>> If gold, her locks are finest gold on ground;
>> If silver, her fair hands are silver sheen:
> But that which fairest is, but few behold,
> Her mind adorned with virtues manifold.

The opening apostrophe, moreover, alludes to *Revelation* 18.10–16 and *Ezekiel* 27–8, which list the same materials among the wealth of a once-beautiful city (Babylon, Tyre). Tyre has claimed 'perfect beauty', but her merchants or suppliers will be terrified by her downfall.[30] In the Biblical exegetic tradition, some of the riches were

---

[29] 'Love Poetry in the Sixteenth Century' *EC* 22 (1972) 377.
[30] See esp. *Ezek.* 27.3 ('O Tyrus, thou hast said, I am of perfect beauty') and 27.6, 12, 16, 22, listing ivory, silver, emeralds and gold. In *Rev.*18.11–12 'the merchants of the earth' are to regret former merchandise of gold, silver, pearls and ivory. For analogues, see Variorum *Minor Poems* 2.424–5: closest is Desportes *Diane* 1.32, where the riches are perhaps allegorized as 'graces'; cf. also G. Marino's elegiac variation, *Rime* (Venice 1608) 1.153: 'le perle, e i rubini e l' ostro, e l' oro/ Dove dove son hor? . . ./ Quante ricchezze un picciol marmo involve,/ Quant' honor. . . . ' W. Drummond of

allegorized as individual virtues; others grouped as the clothing of pre-lapsarian integrity.[31] No doubt some of Spenser's readers would not get farther than the jewels–features matrix of the blazon, and 'but few behold' the additional jewels–virtues matrix. But the uncertain would be helped by his concluding hint: 'her mind adorned with virtues manifold.' Again the conceit depends on complex metaphors. Spenser does not mean that Elizabeth's mind is adorned with virtues as her body with jewels (the proportional metaphor of Aristotle's *Poetics*),[32] since her features do not merely wear, but are, figuratively, the jewels. The implication is rather that *feature* (vehicle) resembles *jewel* (tenor, secondary vehicle) which resembles *virtue* (secondary tenor). In this light, *adorned* may not seem exactly lacking in compression.

The flowers of the *baiser-blason* Sonnet 64, in appearance artlessly sensuous, mere Archimbaldi-like collage, open on inspection into figures of another sort. Behind their swooning synaesthesia, an elusive wit matches each to its feature in unexpected ways. Elizabeth's neck smells like 'a bunch of columbines' because these are white—but also because *collum* means neck. And 'her snowy brows like budded belamours' preserves the continuity of the list by inventing a plausible flower name: the *belamour* is not a bell flower but a love glance, which will bloom as the young lady's 'budded' brow opens.[33] The most

---

[31] Allegorizing *Ezek.* 28.13: 'Thou hast been in Eden the garden of God: every precious stone was in thy garment, the ruby . . . the sapphire, emerald, and the carbuncle and gold [side-note: 'my people Israel which shined as precious stones']' (Geneva). Following *Gen.* 2.10–12, which connects gold and bdellium (Geneva note: 'or pearl') with the River Pison, the 4 rivers of Paradise were correlated with the cardinal virtues (Pison with Prudence): e.g. Philo *De leg. alleg.* 1.19–20, tr. F.H. Colson and G.H. Whitaker vol.1 (New York and London 1929) 187–9; Jerome *Comm. in Ezech.*, Migne *P.L.* 25.270–1 (identifying the jewels of *Ezek.* 28.11 ff., *Is.* 54.11–13, *Rev.* 21 as the sacerdotal stones and Gifts of the Spirit; and (still) Valeriano 21.13; pp.254–5. Also cf.2 *Chron.* 9 on mutual gifts of Solomon and Sheba: esp. v.21 'gold, and silver, ivory'.

[32] 1457 b 11; see Ruthven *The Conceit* 5.

[33] *OED* s.v. *Belamour* 2, e.g. G. Fletcher *Christ's triumph after death* st.48: 'eyes, from whence are shed / Infinite belamours, where to express / His

---

Hawthornden (*The Poetical Works* ed. L.E. Kastner, 2 vols, S.T.S. (Edinburgh and London 1913) 1.52) imitates both Marino and *Amoretti*: 'Those pearls, those rubies, which did breed desire, / Those locks of gold, that purple fair of Tyre, / Are wrapt (aye me!) up in eternal night.' His mention of Tyre shows appreciation of Spenser's Biblical allusion.

complex of the comparisons is also the most erotic: her goodly bosom's resemblance to 'a strawberry bed'. No doubt its main point lies with the concealed nipple-berries; but surely we are also meant to explore the farther association of 'bed' (in a literal sense) with the white pillows to which breasts were commonly likened?[34] Logical analysis in terms of multiple grounds of comparison can hardly be thought adequate. The conceit is a highly impacted metaphor, involving three discourse sets (breasts, nipples), (pillows, bed) and (strawberry bed, berries), with several members submerged. The link between the first vehicle, pillows, and the second tenor, strawberries, depends on no more than the shared word 'bed'. Metaphoric intricacy here allows an unsuggestive lightness of sensuous suggestion.

In a work so various as *Amoretti* we naturally find sonnets of other sorts, from which figurative complexity is absent. But there are also many comparable passages. We need look no farther than a sonnet already discussed for several instances of the obliquity noted in *Amoretti* 64. Subsidiary to the main conceit of *Amoretti* 15 there may be submerged pun in 'her forehead ivory *ween*' ('think', 'fair'); a half-punning aptness to lips in 'rubies *sound*'; and a medical propriety in the choice of sapphires for eyes so good to look at.[35] It would be tasteless to analyse these fugitive graces in logical terms; yet one can scarcely think their semantic structure less complex than that of many a metaphysical conceit. Such incidentally witty decorums are everywhere in *Amoretti*, even though we may think its larger effects, its deeply-meditated complex metaphors, more characteristic of Spenser at his best.

[34] *Les blasons anatomiques du corps féminin . . . composez par plusieurs poètes contemporains* (1550) ed. A.[van] B[ever] (Paris 1907), itself a blazon of erotic blazons: cf. Marot *Blason du beau tétin.* 'Une fraise, ou une cerise,/ Que nul ne voit, ne touche aussi'; and *F.Q.*6.8.42 'Her paps, which like white silken pillows were'.
[35] cf. *Du Bartas* 563: 'Sapphires, cure eyes'. But the correlation of sapphires with eyes was common.

---

love'. Gerard's *Herbal* lists several flowers with *bell* in their name, including one also called Venus' looking-glass. *Polyolbion* 15.170ff. (ed. Hebel et al. 4.307–8), a description of Isis' bridal crown, groups red roses, gillyflowers and pinks as specifically garden flowers, suitable for the bride. On the columbine's theological symbolism see G.Schiller *Iconography of Christian Art* tr. J.Seligman 1 (1971) 51.

Doubled and Circular Metaphors.

Sidney's conceits, if sometimes more dramatic and forceful than Spenser's, are seldom much simpler. *Astrophil and Stella* Sonnet 9 is a characteristic example, possessed of far more complexity than it has been credited with:

> Queen Virtue's court, which some call Stella's face,
>   Prepared by Nature's chiefest furniture,
>   Hath his front built of alabaster pure;
>   Gold is the covering of that stately place.
> The door by which sometimes comes forth her Grace,
>   Red porphir is, which lock of pearl makes sure:
>   Whose porches rich (which name of cheeks endure)
>   Marble mixed red and white do interlace.

A double *allegoria* allows architectural features to stand simultaneously for physical features and for moral qualities. In one, the court is Stella's face, an equation less arbitrary when *face* meant 'façade';[36] in the other, it is virtue's earthly home. That it is the best design of an architect called Nature means both that Stella's face needs no cosmetic embellishing and that she owes her mental qualities to nature in a high philosophical sense.[37] Similarly the court 'hath his front [entrance side] built of alabaster pure' not only because Stella's forehead ('front') is white and smooth, but also because her demeanour is morally pure (the symbolic meaning of alabaster).[38] And the queen ('her Grace') leaving a door of porphiry resembles a spoken grace enunciated by Stella's lips, as well as a favour shown to Astrophil.[39] Such an allegory with double tenors would have been incomprehensible unless some of its component metaphors were already known. Here, Sidney takes for granted not only the familiar blazon motif,

---

[36] *OED* s.v. *Face* sb. III 12 b.

[37] *OED* s.v. *Furniture* I a, the action of accomplishing a design; I b, embellishing; 5 b, intellectual faculties, mental furniture; e.g. Dekker (1609): 'That quality is . . . the only furniture to a courtier'.

[38] *OED* s.v. *Front* II 6; cf. I 1, forehead; I 3 a, demeanour. *Cheeks* could mean the side pieces (cf. 'porches') of a doorway (*OED* 9). Alabaster was the pure receptacle of the ointment of faith: see Raban Maur, in Migne *P.L.* 107.1101-2 on *John* 12.3; and cf. *Old Arcadia* Poem 62 l.80 (ed. Robertson 240; ed. Ringler 88): 'a spotless mine of alabaster'; also Diana's oratory in Chaucer *Knight's T.* I (A) 1910.

[39] *OED* s.v. *Grace* II 8 and 16 b. Grace was a blazon item: see *Les blasons anatomiques* 85.

which correlated a fairly restricted range of precious materials with physical features,[40] but also the allegorical house motif, based on dream symbolism, which correlated architectural and bodily or moral properties.

In addition, schemes linking riches and virtues underlie the thought, as in *Amoretti* 15. But in *Astrophil and Stella* word-plays that clench the various chains of discourse together are more frequent. Sidney's fondness for *antanaclasis, adnominatio* and pun may even be judged excessive: his rhetoric, though brilliant and powerful, lacks something of Spenser's delicacy. In the present sonnet, indeed, the play on *touch* is notorious for its manneristic extremity; without ever, perhaps, having received adequate interpretation:

> The windows now through which this heavenly guest
> Looks over the world, and can find nothing such,
> Which dare claim from those lights the name of best,
> Of touch they are that without touch doth touch,
> Which Cupid's self from Beauty's mine did draw:
> Of touch they are, and poor I am their straw.

The 'lights' or 'windows' that the guest looks out from have been applied to Stella: their black touchstone resembles the darkness of her eyes, which emotionally 'touch' and attract Astrophil as rubbed jet attracts straw by the action of its electrostatic field—only 'without touch', without rubbing, without sexual contact.[41] Perhaps also there is the more bitter implication that Stella affects Astrophil injuriously, that is, touches him, without having any imagination—any 'sense of inward touch'—about his feelings.[42] But all of this lies within the court–face allegory: we should also follow out the allegory of Queen Virtue. In it, the 'lights' are moral lights or examples, and the 'touch' is true touchstone, which 'doth touch' (i.e., tests) and finds the world

---

[40] On the amorous blazon see Ruthven 'The Composite Mistress' (relating it to schemes of planetary gifts); Ringler 410; R.L.Montgomery *Symmetry and Sense: the Poetry of Sir Philip Sidney* (New York 1969) 125; M.B. Ogle 'The Classical Origin and Tradition of Literary Conceits' *Amer. Journ. of Philol.* 34 (1913) 125–52; and above, ch.2 n.10.

[41] See Ringler 463–4, which rightly identifies these touch eyes with Sonn. 91's 'seeing jets' and so detects electrostatically-charged lignite. *OED* s.v. *Touch* sb. II 6, touchstone; vb I 24, stir the feelings; sb. II 11, magnetizing; vb I 6 c, magnetize by rubbing with a magnet; sb. I I a, b, physical touch, sexual contact. See Alan Sinfield 'Sexual Puns in *Astrophil and Stella*' *EC* 24 (1974) 346.

[42] *OED* s.v. *Touch* vb I 7, affect injuriously; sb. III 14, moral perception.

around to be of inferior metal.[43] The final couplet may well introduce a farther application, with Cupid igniting Astrophil's straw, by 'lights' from touch-powder, to kindle the familiar fire of passion.[44] But in any event the sestet clearly offers alternative rather than complementary grounds for comparison. Doubling of metaphors by *antanaclasis* and pun, a favourite local device with Sidney, here determines the overall effect. We have to choose between a virtuously testing and a magnetically attractive Stella, with some sense of unresolved contradiction.[45] Is this really a Court of Virtue or (as Cupid's participation suggests) a Court of Love? The building materials confirm the latter identification: they would once have been recognizable as quarried from the pseudo-Chaucerian *Court of love*.[46] Yet the tone will not easily allow reconciliation of the two aspects in terms of the Venus–Virgo or any such composite figure. On the contrary, once 'Queen Virtue' is understood dramatically, like Astrophil's sarcasm, other phrases too may acquire ironic force. Do 'some' call Stella's virtue *only* her 'face' or outward show?[47] Does Astrophil consciously imagine theological grace leaving Stella as she grants him a favour? Does he regard her as not just 'stately' but vain, incapable as she is of seeing anything her superior? At least in Astrophil's view the choice of an opaque material for the windows (Cupid's doing, not Nature's) may be a little ridiculous. No wonder Queen Virtue can see so little.[48]

Appreciation of *Astrophil and Stella* 1 depends no less heavily on multiple relations of tenor and vehicle. No reader will get far without grasping that poetical composition is simultaneously allegorized as

[43] *OED* s.v. *Light* sb. 8 a, b, moral luminary, *Touch* vb 1 8 a, test the fineness of (esp. gold or silver). Jet was also used as a test in the ancient guilt-divining ritual of axinomancy.

[44] *OED* s.v. *Light* sb. 14 a, spark igniting any combustible substance (earliest ex. 1684); s.v. *Touch* sb. IV 21, touch-powder; and s.v. *Touch-powder*.

[45] B. Twyne's contemporary misreading (Bodl. CCC. MS. 263 fols 114b–120, quoted Ringler 463–4) shows him ready to fault the reasoning—perhaps Astrophil's, however, not Sidney's.

[46] Which Sidney would read in Stowe's Chaucer (1561) fol. 348 ff. See *Chaucerian and other Pieces* ed. W. W. Skeat (Oxford 1897) 411.

[47] *OED* s.v. *Face* sb. II 10, outward show; factitious appearance; pretence.

[48] In confirmation, 'Gold is the covering of that stately place' indicates a House of Pride (below, 119); cf. too 'windows of kindness', *Quia amore langueo* st. 13. But contrast Is. 54.11–12, a key text for the blazon subgenre: 'I will make thy windows of emeralds [A.V. 'agates'], and thy gates shining stones' (Geneva).

childbirth ('came forth . . . great with child') and as stumbling ('came halting . . . wanting Invention's stay'). The first *allegoria* develops a traditional personification of Nature as the mother of Art by making Invention (also a traditional mother of Art) a would-be assistant at the birth, prevented from helping by Study (only a step-mother, since she unlike Nature cannot produce anything new).[49] The second *allegoria* presents the words associated with Study. They stumble, whether from *vieux-jeux* decrepitude or unsteady inexperience, against the obstacle of other poets' irrelevant models (metrical 'feet').[50] Invention, again, cannot help, inhibited as she is by the daunting regime of laborious Study. We have to notice at least the entanglement of these metaphors, before we can appreciate Astrophil's passion, let alone Sidney's art:

> But words came halting forth, wanting Invention's stay,
> Invention, Nature's child, fled step-dame Study's blows,
> And others' feet still seemed but strangers in my way.
> Thus great with child to speak, and helpless in my throes,
> Biting my truant pen, beating my self for spite,
> 'Fool,' said my Muse to me, 'Look in thy heart and write.'

Two or more discourse sets (childbirth and first or second childhood) separately resemble Astrophil's difficulties of expression when he allows Invention to be neglected. The vehicular chains are linked by pun ('came forth'), by shared personifications ('Study', 'Invention'), and perhaps by a scheme of Ages of Man corresponding to stages of composition in the tenor. But they remain distinct metaphors, as their non-sequential arrangement—with postnatal tripping followed by throes of childbirth—makes plain. Here, figurative structure is more than a display of Sidney's penchant for ambiguity: it deliberately mimes the impatient disorder of Astrophil's mind.[51]

---

[49] On Natura and Invenzione as mothers of art in Vasari, see Panofsky *Renaissance* 31 n.2. Sidney may follow Ficino's genealogy, in which Natura's first-remove images claim seniority both to *natura naturata* and to art's imitations: Plato *Opera omnia additis Marsilii Ficini . . . commentariis* (Basel 1561) 683, the fine passage beginning 'ascende age Platonice contemplator . . . ad naturam formarum ciusmodi genetricem'. By this metaphysic, the poet's image of Stella had independent status.

[50] The reference to the sonnet's un-English alexandrines makes a further pun.

[51] Taine's notorious account of *Astrophil and Stella* as the expression of Sidney's obsession ('in every extreme passion ordinary laws are reversed. . . . Our logic cannot pass judgment on it. . . . Common sense and good

We have discussed only two forms of compound metaphor: Spenser's complex embedded conceits, and Sidney's doubled vehicles or tenors. But other forms were also cultivated. Michael Drayton, in particular, produced a great variety, including multiple conceits, and a circular complex type in which the distant vehicle returns to literal tenor discourse:

> All fence the tree which serveth for a shade,
>> Whose great grown body doth repulse the wind,
> Until his wasteful branches do invade,
>> The straighter plants, and them in prison bind,
>> Then like a foul devower of his kind:
> Unto his root all put their hands to hew,
>> Whose roomth but hinder other which would grow.[52]

This *allegoria* for human orgulousness obviously becomes complex metaphor when the figurative tree is itself likened, because of its habit, to a human traitor. Similarly, *invade* and *prison* introduce complex metaphors, since they are figurative words so far as arboreal discourse is concerned. However, they also return to literal discourse, in which powerful barons might well invade and imprison. Several circular conceits come within the few stanzas narrating Edward's subterranean mission. Perhaps the finest is an evocation of

> These gloomy lamps, by which they on were led,
>> Making their shadows follow at their back,
> Which like to mourners, wait upon the dead,
>> And as the dead, so are they ugly black,
>> Like to the dreadful images of wrack;
> These poor dim-burning lights, as all amazed,
>> As those deformed shades whereon they gazed.[53]

Here *wrack*, revenge, is quite literally the journey's purpose, so that the second vehicle reverts to the first tenor. The recursive comparisons of *Mortimeriados* sometimes achieve remarkable compression, as in the hyperbole praising the queen: 'That lily hand, rich Nature's

---

[52] *Mortimeriados* 2282–5, ed. Hebel et al. 1.374. Either *devower = devourer*, or it means 'one who devows, i.e., gives up by oath, sacrifices'. A typical instance of multiple comparisons comes at *Mortimeriados* 2423 ff., ed. Hebel et al. 1.378.
[53] ibid. 2465–71, Hebel 1.379.

---

language cannot penetrate') would not be ridiculous, if we read 'Astrophil' for 'Sidney' (*History of English Literature* tr. H. van Laun 1 (Edinburgh 1873) 169. For a recent discussion see R. A. Lanham '*Astrophil and Stella:* Pure and Impure Persuasion' *ELR* 2 (1972) 100–2.

wedding glove'.[54] To say that such poetry contents the eye is true, but it is also a staggering oversimplification.

It would not be difficult to carry this review of metaphoric types a great deal father. But we must beware: classifying Elizabethan conceits easily works against their grain of unexpectedness, their proclivity to surprise precisely by the copiousness of their formal obliquity.

The Metaphysical Conceit.

Compound metaphors are less characteristic of Metaphysical poetry. Not that the poets who devised Metaphysical conceits lacked the power of subtle thought. But this sort of complexity is not typically a feature of their work. On the contrary, the simplicity of figurative structure must strike anyone who thinks about Metaphysical conceits in the light of the foregoing, and make him wonder whether their design may not intend a relatively immediate effect. Donne's comparison of souls to gold leaf in *A valediction: forbidding mourning* may be far-fetched, but the fetching offers little poetical difficulty. Logical ingenuity easily puzzles it out. There is one tenor, the lovers' conjoined soul suffering blows of physical separation; and one vehicle, gold beaten into a fine but extensive form. Even if 'airy' (light; immaterial) suggests the purified condition of the extended soul,[55] this does not constitute a second tenor, only a farther ground of resemblance. A far-fetched comparison usually requires several grounds to make it good: here, absence of a 'breach' (break-up of friendly relations: physical fracture); 'expansion';[56] and the heaviness and purposefulness of the maker's blows.

In the conceit of the compasses immediately after, grounds of comparison are more numerous still. They include firmness of connection (united souls: 'stiff . . . compasses'); responsiveness of the fixed member; disparity of motions (homekeeping and travelling: 'sit . . . roam'); and final reunion (home-coming: closing of the compasses). But all belong to a single system of relations between

[54] ibid. 2504, Hebel 1.380.

[55] *John Donne: The Complete English Poems* ed. A.J.Smith (Harmondsworth 1971) 405–6: 'their love will be so refined by absence as to pass beyond the highest condition of material nature to the still more exalted quality of air or spirit.' See *OED* s.v. *Airy* II 5, e.g. Trevisa (1398): 'the pure and airy matter'.

[56] *OED* s.v. *Expansure* (= *Expansion*), e.g. *Sir G. Goosecap* (1606): 'my immortal part admits expansure.'

souls and compasses. The effect, indeed, very much depends on the fact that details of the compass action come in unbroken sequential order. (Earl Miner goes so far as to say 'the Metaphysical poets were more interested in the vehicles than in the tenors of their metaphors'.[57]) The rhetorical structure, as a result, remains simple and easily grasped, in spite of a series of more or less subdued puns: 'fixed'; 'sits'; 'hearkens after' (inquires after: has relation to); 'grows erect' (uplifted with expectation: vertical); 'obliquely' (geometrical and moral senses); and 'firmness'.[58] The ordered set of compass particulars is matched with a set of moral properties, almost as an emblem's iconology is explained item by item.[59] This conceit of Donne's, an awkward one for the present argument, happens to use an actual emblem, the completing of a circle, which traditionally symbolized Constancy or sometimes the perfection of divine love;[60] so that it comes close to having a doubled tenor. Even so, this farther meaning relates to the whole action of the compasses, not to any of its parts. And it is not really a separate meaning: the lovers' constancy is an instance of Constancy (and an image of divine love); from one point of view the conceit only expands the emblem. In this case, as with many of the conceits we call Metaphysical, the figurative structure seems to be simplified by a baroque unification or intensification of effect.

Most of Donne's secular conceits—including intermediate examples such as those in *Air and angels*—have the simplest of figurative structures. On the other hand, his divine poems have often fairly complex metaphors. And seventeenth-century religious poetry in

[57] *The Metaphysical Mode from Donne to Cowley* (Princeton, N.J. 1969) 143.
[58] *OED* s.v. *Hearken* 6, e.g. *Mucho Ado* 5.1.216 'Hearken after their offence' and 9, only ex. Pope *Essay on Man* 4.40 'leans and hearkens to the kind'; *Erect* A 3, 1; *Oblique* 1, 4 (deviating from right conduct).
[59] On this tendency cf. Miner 132.
[60] *The Elegies and The Songs and Sonnets* ed. H. Gardner (Oxford 1965) 189–90 cites Plantin's LABORE ET CONSTANTIA emblem, Guarini and Hall; cf. J. Lederer 'John Donne and the Emblematic Practice' *RES* 22 (1946); R. Skelton in *Elizabethan Poetry* ed. Brown and Harris 216 and pl. 2 (Wither's LABORE ET CONSTANTIA); Henkel and Schöne col. 1420 (LABORE ET CONSTANTIA) and col. 6 (SINE FINE, from Heinsius and Valeriano). J. Freccero 'Donne's "Valediction: Forbidding Mourning"' *ELH* 30 (1963) 335–76 discloses additional alchemical and astrological symbolisms; suggesting that the compasses describe the *Timaeus* spiral. On the esoteric character of emblematic conceits see Yates 'The Emblematic Conceit' 101–21; Ruthven *The Conceit* 35–7.

general shares this tendency; perhaps because meditation on familiar symbols allowed and encouraged it. Typological conceits, for example, commonly involve compound metaphor, since they deploy two additional discourse sets (Old Testament antitype and New Testament type) in relation to the immediate topic.[61] Both Herbert's and Donne's divine poems can have quite complex figures; though as often as not these have escaped notice. A familiar instance is Donne's *Batter my heart*, with its combination of siege and marriage metaphors, and its multiple comparisons in the opening lines:

> Batter my heart, three personed God; for, you
> As yet but knock, breathe, shine, and seek to mend;
> That I may rise, and stand, o'erthrow me, and bend
> Your force, break, blow, burn and make me new.

Here the *asyndeton* 'knock, breathe, shine' not only develops a metaphor of polishing and repair in exact contrast with the more active 'break, blow, burn', but also implies other quite distinct metaphors. *Knock* in the sense 'strike the breast penitentially' may once have been as obvious as 'knock up, summon' and 'knock together', idioms not ineluctably represented by their first segment.[62] If the verbs are distributed between the persons of the 'three personed God' (among whom the Light of the World might be expected to shine, and the Spirit or *pneuma* to breathe), farther compound comparisons may be involved.[63] But one could not conscientiously say that even here the sonnet turns on complex figures: its redundancy or self-confirmatory forms are of a less demanding order, its rhetoric simple and insistent enough for the point to be unmistakeable.

In secular Metaphysical poems, figurative complexity is far less often met. Perhaps the dramatic character, certainly the determined novelty of a work such as Donne's *Songs and Sonnets*, has quite a different tendency. Indeed, if we were to construct a model Metaphysical conceit, we would not specify complexity of comparison. The specification would be a single tenor and a single vehicle, related by

[61] ibid. 43–4.
[62] *OED* s.v. Knock v. 1 1 b, strike upon the breast; e.g. Strype (1562): 'divers communicants . . . superstitiously both kneel and knock' and Babington (1583); 1 6 d, 11 16 f, rouse or summon; 11 14 c, 16 d, put together hastily; cf. Miller 131.
[63] For a theory of Trinitarian structure in *Batter my heart*, arrived at on independent grounds, see D. K. Cornelius 'Donne's *Holy Sonnet 14*' *Explicator* 24.3 (1966) no. 25.

a single system of analogies. Whether the grounds of similarity are numerous or the comparison oilstoned down to one Clevelandish catachresis; whether the things compared are briefly mentioned or un-packed into many items and aspects on each side, wittily interconnec-ted by puns, ambiguities and other word-plays: at all events an overall simplicity of tropic structure prevails. The simplicity may strike us less than the difficulties and ingenuities. But reflection dis-covers that overt dialectical subtleties present in the end less of an obstacle than implicit rhetorical complexities, which may go un-noticed. Perhaps Thomas Fuller was making a not dissimilar point when he wrote of Cleveland's 'difficult plainness', and claimed that his metaphors were 'plain at the considering thereof'. Such metaphors can, as it were, be solved. This limited difficulty may have something to do with the accessibility of the Metaphysical style. Its problems look, at least, as if they can be resolved by a close reading of what we carelessly refer to as 'the words on the page'.

In itself this may do little harm. So far as sixteenth-century poetry is concerned, however, the misconception of comparative easiness has proved fatal to appreciation. The comparison is doubly wrong. In the earlier period, wider reliance on familiar metaphors in fact made pos-sible more complex figurative construction. And secondly, these once familiar metaphors have themselves, in some cases, become obscure. When shared associations are severed, when the metaphoric vocu-bulary is forgotten, communication may break down and leave us un-impressed by poetry of an apparently jejune simplicity.

Renaissance Theories of Metaphor.

It would be foolish to hope for much confirmation of the point I have been making, in Renaissance literary theory. We cannot expect Elizabethan theorists to have the same problems and interests as we have. The only relevant material has been found in seventeenth-century discussions of such aspects of the *concetto* as correspondence and acuity. However, we should allow for the retrospective relation of formal theory to innovating practice. Earlier interest shows clearly enough, if not formally, in the self-consciousness of Elizabethan conceits ('Long-while I sought to what I might compare/Those powerful eyes'[64]); in the discrimination with which they overgo or

[64] *Amoretti* 9; cf. Shakespeare *Sonnets* 18 'Shall I compare thee to a summer's day?'

invert conventional comparisons ('black wires grow on her head'[65]); and in the notes which encourage connoisseurship in variations of a metaphor.[66] Moreover, the rhetoricians differentiated various sorts of 'translative' or comparing figures—*catachresis, metonymia, antonamasia, epitheton*—that are now lumped together as 'metaphor'. And readers of Rosemond Tuve's *Elizabethan and Metaphysical Imagery* (esp. pp. 281–330) will know that Tudor as well as Stuart concettists habitually distinguished logical grounds of similarity. Can they have done so without separating the things compared?

Earlier rhetoricians, I suspect, came close to the matter of conceit structure in their treatments of *allegoria* or *inversio*, a figure defined as 'long and perpetual metaphor'.[67] They made a distinction between metaphors with a continuous vehicle chain ('full allegory') and 'another manner of allegory not full, but mixed, as he that wrate thus: "The clouds of care have covered all my coast".'[68] Here an irruption of the tenor explains 'clouds', which in full allegory 'should not be discovered'. This example of Puttenham's shows a common type of interruption of vehicular discourse, named by Christine Brooke-Rose 'the genitive link'.[69] In the same way, Peacham finds commixed allegory in *Matthew* 3.12, 'He . . . will burn the chaff with unquenchable fire': the epithet 'unquenchable' is not a member of the agricultural discourse set, but belongs to the tenor of everlasting punishment.[70] And John Hoskins shows a clear grasp of the concept

[65] ibid. 130. For the avoidance of outworn comparison cf. Ronsard *Sonets pour Hélène* 2.12 ('Je ne veux comparer tes beautez à la Lune'). On burlesque conceits see Ruthven *The Conceit* 25 ff.; K. M. Wilson *Shakespeare's Sugared Sonnets* (New York 1974).

[66] e.g. T. Watson's notes in *The passionate century of love* (1582) and the glosses in Spenser *S.C.* (1579). Also cf. Tesauro's instructions for generating witty metaphors from familiar ones, discussed S. L. Bethell 'The Nature of Metaphysical Wit' reptd *Discussions of John Donne* ed. F. Kermode (Boston 1962) 141–2.

[67] Puttenham 3.18; ed. Willcock and Walker 187. For similar definitions see L. A. Sonnino *A Handbook to Sixteenth-Century Rhetoric* (1968) 120–1; or Spenser's Letter to Raleigh: 'continued allegory, or dark conceit'.

[68] Puttenham 3.18; ed. Willock and Walker 188.

[69] *A Grammar of Metaphor* (1958) 19: 'Metaphor by genitive apposition (the fire of love)'.

[70] H. Peacham *The garden of eloquence* (1577), facs. ed. R. C. Alston (Menston 1971) sig. D 2r 'The sense hereof is, that Christ in the last judgement . . . shall separate the good from the bad . . . and deliver the wicked, to everlasting pains.' Interestingly, Peacham felt able to give a Ciceronian example in translation: 'he mingled the allegory, when he said the waves of conscience.'

of field of discourse in his comment on *Arcadia* (1590) fol. 116v ('But when that wish had once his ensign in his mind, then followed whole squadrons of longings, that so it might be a main battle of mislikings and repinings against their creation'): '*Ensigns, squadrons, main battle,*— metaphors still derived from the same thing [as] at first, war'.[71] Such an approach would not be unconducive to appreciation of Elizabethan compound and multiple metaphors. But inevitably practice outstripped theory. A terminology designed to identify local rhetorical effects was poorly adapted for describing more pervasive and elusive figurative shadings.

In a less rhetorical way, theorists as diverse as Alciati, Giordano Bruno and Abraham Fraunce considered metaphor in relation to the emblem or device. Bruno's *Gli eroici furori* is discussed from this point of view by Frances Yates in a famous article contrasting the earlier Petrarchist conceit with a later, more 'baroque' form, manifested in Sidney and Drayton, which she likens to an allegorical treatment of Petrarchan imagery. The comparison is a good one. It draws attention to a kind of secondary metaphor mentioned by several contemporary theorists, among whom one might particularly notice Abraham Fraunce. For Fraunce the archetypal poem is the *Song of Solomon*, a work 'altogether mystical and allegorical':

> Poetical songs are galleries set forth with variety of pictures, to hold every man's eyes, gardens stored with flowers of sundry savours, to delight every man's sense, orchards furnished with all kinds of fruit, to please every man's mouth. He that is but of a mean conceit, hath a pleasant and plausible narration . . . to feed his rural humour. They, whose capacity is such, as that they can reach somewhat further than the external discourse and history, shall find a moral sense included therein, extolling virtue. . . .[72]

It was a theoretical position such as this that produced the Elizabethan form of emblematic blazon, which as we have seen was very different

---

[71] *Directions for speech and style* ed. H. H. Hudson (Princeton, N.J. 1935) 9. The comment on a *similitudo* or *allegoria* in *Arcadia* (1590) fol. 326 ('Philoclea was so environed with sweet rivers of virtue as that she could neither be battered nor undermined') shows awareness of two sets of 'terms': '*Philoclea's virtue*, the proper [*sc.* literal] terms of the one part; *environed, rivers, battered, undermined,* the terms of the other part; all these terms in one sentence and it is an allegory.'

[72] A. Fraunce *The third part of the Countess of Pembroke's Ivychurch* (1592) 4. See Yates 'The Emblematic Conceit'.

from that of Petrarch. The emblematic conceit, however, was as much a mannerist as a baroque feature. And it was not characteristic of secular Metaphysical poetry.

In the seventeenth century, Elizabethan essays at legitimizing mixed *allegoria* and compound or multiple metaphor seem not to have been much followed up. Perhaps this is to be connected with a movement of taste, in the England of Jonson and Donne, to a more classical norm. Classical tastes have generally preferred 'consistency' of metaphor and disliked broken or entangled or profusely festooned chains of discourse. In the Scottish Enlightenment Hugh Blair faulted Pope for 'confused mixtures of metaphorical and plain language', and even more for making 'two different metaphors meet on one object'. He formulated a rule 'for examining the propriety of metaphors': the critic was to visualize the parts and so test for 'inconsistent circumstances'. In such a test Shakespeare could only be put down as a gross violator of Quintilian's taboo.[73] We may smile; but in our own century Cuningham emended Shakespeare, and Robert Bridges Hopkins, on the basis of 'necessary continuity of metaphors'. They are rightly castigated by Professor Leavis: 'Good metaphor need not be a matter of consistently worked out analogy or point-for-point parallel'.[74]

Shakespeare's Sonnet 97.

The change of taste sketched above has more critical bearings than I can hope to indicate in this chapter. But something of its import appears when we turn to Shakespeare, the greatest poet who wrote in the earlier figurative manner. Except that he is quicker and more intense, he may be closely compared with Spenser (*pace* Hunter) so far as exploring involved figurative relations is concerned. Reluctance to see this has led to very much confusion about Shakespeare's imagery. Even J. B. Leishman could reject the metaphors of Sonnet 97, although 'beautiful in themselves and even unforgettable', because they 'contradict and conflict with one another at almost every point, and the more closely one examines the whole passage the more hopelessly

---

[73] H. Blair *Lectures on Rhetoric and Belles Lettres* (1824) Lect. 15, pp. 187–8; cf Index s.v. *Pope.* Quintilian's condemnation of mixed metaphor (*Inst.* 8.6.50), misunderstood in the 18th cent., referred to vehicles from incongruous fields of discourse. The requirement was that compound metaphors should be appropriate, not continuous. Indeed, *Inst.* 8.6.47–9 provided a model for Renaissance accounts of mixed allegory.
[74] F. R. Leavis *New Bearings in English Poetry* (1932) 192.

incoherent it appears'.[75] This objection follows from a preference for
the Metaphysical metaphor, with its single consistent system of correspondences. But one can think of classical critics who would agree;
it was Ben Jonson who applied Augustus' criticism of Haterius to
Shakespeare: *sufflaminandus erat*.[76]

The incoherence seemed to Leishman to arise from contradictory
personifications: Spring ('the prime'), Summer and Autumn:

How like a winter hath my absence been
From thee, the pleasure of the fleeting year?
What freezings have I felt, what dark days seen?
What old December's bareness every where?
And yet this time removed was summer's time,
The teeming Autumn big with rich increase,
Bearing the wanton burden of the prime,
Like widowed wombs after their lords' decease:
Yet this abundant issue seemed to me,
But hope of orphans, and unfathered fruit,
For Summer and his pleasures wait on thee,
And thou away, the very birds are mute.
Or if they sing, 'tis with so dull a cheer,
That leaves look pale, dreading the winter's near.

Is this not in effect to write that it was summer, that Autumn was at
the same time pregnant by her dead husband Spring, but that only
orphans could be hoped for, because her husband Summer had gone
away? To imply that 'Autumn's children will be fatherless because
Summer has departed' is weak, since 'Summer always *has* departed
before Autumn's children are born.'[77] The notion of simultaneous
seasons may seem less ridiculous if one recalls the Ovidian *Horae*. But
Leishman's difficulty really arises, as often with Shakespeare, from not
disengaging compound relations of tenor and vehicle.

The first quatrain develops a single *allegoria* or extended metaphor,

[75] J.B.Leishman *Themes and Variations in Shakespeare's Sonnets* (1963) 191;
cf. C.K.Pooler *Sonnets* (1918), and C.L.Barber in *Elizabethan Poetry* ed.
P.J.Alpers (1967) 307. P.Cruttwell, like Leishman, connects the *Sonnets*
with Metaphysical poetry, in *The Shakespearean Moment and its Place in the
Poetry of the Seventeenth Century* (1954). But Hunter firmly distinguishes
Shakespearean and Metaphysical styles: see 'The Dramatic Technique of
Shakespeare's Sonnets' *EC* 3 (1953) 161 and cf. Miner 155–6.
[76] ed. Herford and Simpson 8.584. The criticism referred originally to
'uncontrolled' *figures*: see Seneca *Controv.* 4 Pref. 7–11.
[77] Leishman 191, 193.

in which winter's properties are a vehicle conveying the poet's loss of 'the pleasure of the fleeting year'. This phrase has been taken as a *pronominatio* for summer. But it might as well be the sun whose absence in winter means 'freezings', 'dark days' and 'bareness' (or 'barrenness').[78] In any event, the comparison of absence and winter returns later in 'Summer and his pleasures wait on thee . . . ': as the poet's sun, the beloved is not just summer, but lord of summer.[79]

In the second quatrain, a new comparison is introduced, without inconsistency, however. The time of absence, though it seemed like winter, actually fell in very different seasons: 'summer's time' (i.e. summer-time, or possibly Summer's time of childbirth) and 'teeming Autumn', personified as a woman bearing a child.[80] This child is the 'wanton burden of the prime' not because Spring is the father, but because natural growth is quickened by the action of the sun in his prime or period of greatest vigour, *summer*.[81] The personification of Autumn depends on a series of word-plays on human and agricultural meanings. Thus *wanton* meant 'luxuriant' as well as 'frolicsome'; *teeming* 'pregnant' as well as 'sprouting'; while *increase* and *burden* referred both to crops and child. Even *Autumn*, besides the personification, could signify 'crops'—opening up a *prolepsis* through *big* to future harvests.[82] From one point of view the figure is 'mixed allegory', since *rich* applies only to crops, not to human increase. The difficulty

---

[78] The 1609 spelling *barenesse* could probably indicate either. On the identification of sun and beloved, see Lever 222–3.

[79] cf. the festive titles Summer Lord and Harvest Lord, *OED* s.v. *Lord* 14 a, *Harvest* sb.7; and see C. L. Barber *Shakespeare's Festive Comedy* (Princeton, N.J. 1959) Index s.v. *Summer Lord and Lady*. Also cf. Cartari 43–4 on Sol as padrone de' tempi. Some of the confusion may arise from 'summer and his'. This form need imply no personification: *his* could be used for ModE. *its*.

[80] For 'summer's time' = Summer's time of childbirth, see *OED* s.v. *Time* 11 15 b (but usually with pron.). Not 'time of death', as E. C. Evans in *RES* n.s. 14 (1963)—an otherwise cogent note.

[81] T. G. Tucker's edn of the *Sonnets* takes *prime* as 'early summer, the year in its young manhood.' See *OED* s.v. *Prime* sb.[1] 111 9 a, b, the state of greatest vigour, most flourishing state; e.g. R. Johnson (1603): 'they are only for the owner's pastime in the prime of summer'.

[82] *OED* s.v. *Wanton* A 7, profuse in growth, luxuriant, rank (e.g. Shakespeare *M.N.D.* 2.1.99: 'the quaint mazes in the wanton green'); s.v. *Teeming* ppl.a. 1 a, pregnant, 1 b, germinating, sprouting (earliest ex. 1704), 2, fertile, prolific (e.g. Shakespeare *R.2* 2.1.51 'this teeming womb'); *Autumn* 1 b, the fruits of autumn, harvest (earliest ex. Milton *Par. Lost* 5.394).

whether Autumn's issue is already born[83] seems unnecessary so far as the crops are concerned—particularly since the summer season ran from solstice (13 June) to equinox (14 September). Harvest not only took place in August but was often associated with that summer month, whereas *fruit* was associated with autumn: 'Aestivo segetes, Autumno mitia poma'.[84] Embedded within the childbirth metaphor, however, is a secondary, compound comparison. Mother Autumn bears 'like widowed wombs after their lords' decease'. As the change to plural indicates, these wombs belong to a distinct discourse set. Autumn is *like* the widows, and cannot therefore herself be one. Confusion of the primary and secondary vehicles has led to the error that Autumn's husband is deceased. But Shakespeare's meaning is different: namely, that Autumn's continuing fertility during the absence of the beloved is as heartbreakingly poignant *as if it were* the pregnancy of a widow.

The next lines have given trouble because they intersect all three discourse sets. Yet, writes Shakespeare, this issue (literally crops, figuratively Autumn's offspring, the first vehicle), however abundant, offered no consolation, but seemed like hope of orphans: Autumn's offspring are not literally orphans but *like* orphans (second vehicle). Again, in 'unfathered fruit' the epithet in the sense 'deprived of a father' (*OED* a²) belongs to the bereavement discourse set, in the sense 'illegitimate' (*OED* a¹) to the wanton first vehicle; but the punning *fruit*, while continuing the personification ('fruit of the womb'),[85] returns to the vegetable fruit of literal discourse. The fruit seems to have no father because summer's lord, the poet's sunlike beloved, is away; and since the phenomena of summer *wait on* (accompany, wait for, even 'place their hopes in')[86] him, his absence makes the birds mute or dull. At this the leaves grow pale (as in autumn when the literal sun withdraws), wrongly dreading the dull song as a sign of winter's proximity—as if it really were 'old December'. What feeling hyperboles, what sensitivity to the ambiguous moods of a sadly impending seasonal transition, must be missed, if this sonnet's

---

[83] Settled by W. G. Ingram and T. Redpath in favour of an antenatal situation: see *Shakespeare's Sonnets* (1964) 222.

[84] *Carmina illustrium poetarum Italorum* 11 vols (Florence 1719) 2.99. T. Tusser *Five hundred points of good husbandry* (1573) ed. W. Payne and S. J. Herrtage (1878) 124–37 treats harvest under August.

[85] *OED* s.v. *Fruit* sb. 6, offspring, fruit of the womb; Biblical diction (e.g. Shakespeare *3 H.6* 4.4.24 'King Edward's fruit'). [86] *OED* 14 h, n.

involved comparisons are all reduced to a single, botched, Metaphysical conceit.

One example will not usually carry much weight. But the imagery of Sonnet 97, it must be conceded, is in a high degree characteristic of the *Sonnets* as a whole. And when we turn to the plays (which Jonson would chiefly have in mind) we discover them to be crowded with complex figures. Think of the involved comparison in Macbeth's 'Come seeling night' speech (3.2.46 ff.), or Hamlet's 'To be or not to be' soliloquy, or almost any other familiar passage. Even in *Coriolanus*, whose rhetoric is comparatively spare, we find such images as 'the honoured mould/ Wherein this trunk was framed' (5.3.23). If the evidence were fully considered, I believe we should almost have to call the conceit with embedded or double comparisons the Shakespearean Conceit.[87] This is not quite to say, however, that Shakespeare's conceits in the Elizabethan manner must be regarded as antiquated survivals. We may recognize some diachronic extension of the various modes of conceit. One, which we found in examples from Spenser, Sidney, and Shakespeare, could be traced also in Herbert, Donne (the Divine Poems), and Milton. Another, the 'Metaphysical' mode characteristic of Donne (*Songs and Sonnets*) and his imitators, appeared much earlier, for example in the Petrarchists. The different styles not only overlapped, but coexisted in the same author. Nevertheless, a broad movement is observable, around 1600, in the style of extended metaphors. This was not a movement from simple to complex. It would be nearer the truth (though still an oversimplification) to say that one sort of complexity, suitable for sustained meditation and large imaginative construction, gave way to another sort, adaptable to quick striking effects. The witty, immediate point of the Metaphysical conceit might be accompanied by less immediate, more demanding figurative effects. Or it might not.

[87] Others have formed similar conclusions; see e.g. the discussion of Sonn. 146's 'alternative vehicles' and doubly submerged metaphor, Miller 132.

6

The Locality of Jonson's
To Penshurst

═══

Few problems of interpretation are more resistant to solution, particularly by the critical approach most cultivated during the last few decades, than that presented by a difficult poem with seemingly plain language and simple forms. There are no obvious local difficulties to solve nor immediate evocations to follow up, so that the surface seems too polished, even too featureless, to afford points of entry. Yet the poem as a whole is somehow obscure. We are inclined now to see such cases, which often come up in Tudor and Stuart poetry, as problems of kind. The obstacle to appreciation is our ignorance of the precise genre. We do not know, perhaps, what works to relate the problem poem to, what innovation or modification it introduces, what conventions it follows or breaks, what motifs it uses or combines. We do not, as it were, know how to take it.

The generic features of a poem can come to seem blurred or hard to identify in a variety of ways. Contributory genres may have suffered extinction so that the poem's preceding congeners are no longer recognizable as a group: the river epithalamium, for example, was an important type in Tudor landscape poetry, forming a tradition incorporated in *Prothalamion*, and still contributing to Ben Jonson's *To Penshurst*. Again, enjoyment through genre is much bound up with appreciation of allusion and creative imitation. From this point of view it is unfortunate that much Tudor manuscript poetry has been lost; and that the Neolatin or vernacular Continental models emulated by Elizabethan poets might as well be lost, for all the effect they have on criticism. Thomas Watson's headnotes are continually urging us to compare his conceits with those of some Stephanus Forcatulus or Hercules Strozza or Gervasius Sepinus. Uncertainty of allusion is a great problem with Tudor and Stuart poetry. We usually think of allusion as a constituent that only begins to matter with Dryden and the Augustan canon that has continued in force more or less into our own time. But Spenser's poetry is highly allusive; and so, I believe, is Jonson's.

Another reason why generic register sometimes proves elusive is that genres may have quite specific social matrices. With poems written at a time of individual patronage, when the concept of readership was highly specialized, context often seems lacking. In English literature this problem becomes most acute around 1600.

Jonson's *To Penshurst,* which shows several of these factors, is the subject of the present chapter. There are advantages in choosing this work, even though it lies a little outside the confines of Tudor poetry. Indeed, it positively challenges consideration in the present connection, since it is supposed to be a paradigmatic example of the creation of a new genre. As we shall see, this does not mean that it sprang fully formed, without antecedents, but rather that Jonson decisively reassembled a fresh combination of elements. On the other hand, *To Penshurst* is late enough, and its classical cast sufficiently pronounced, for the allusions and imitations to be relatively accessible. Its constituent genres and motifs are predominantly ancient; even though there proves to be more of a Renaissance contribution than we might have expected.

To Penshurst first appeared in print as the second poem of Ben Jonson's *The forest,* in 1612. At that time the system of personal patronage, in spite of the increasing importance of monetary contracts and of public patronage, had still its full force,[1] and this older system, which could spur or check a poet's genius, threaten or sustain his integrity, brought out the best in Jonson. Indeed, addresses to patrons figure among his greatest poems. They have a judiciousness and independence that similar poems of Donne's, for example, arguably lack. A fine work in its own right, *To Penshurst* also established an emergent English genre, the country-house poem, which was adumbrated only indistinctly in Leland's *Cygnea cantio,* the Latin verses of Jonson's old schoolmaster Camden, or Spenser's emblematic houses and topographical passages, on the one hand, and in Martial's epigrams, Horace's *Beatus ille,* or Ausonius' *De Mosella,* on the other.[2] The pattern

---

[1] See P. Thomson 'The Literature of Patronage, 1580–1630' *EC* 2 (1952), qualified ibid. 3 (1953) 109, 120; J. Buxton *Sir Philip Sidney and the English Renaissance* (1954); E. Rosenberg *Leicester: Patron of Letters* (New York 1955).
[2] G. R. Hibbard, *JWI* 19 (1956), outlines the genre but leaves historical interpretation to C. Molesworth, *Genre* 1 (1968). See also R. Gill *Happy Rural Seat* (New Haven and London 1972) 227 ff. I. Rivers *The Poetry of Conservatism*

of imitation shows that subsequently the kind was directly generated by *To Penshurst* and *To Sir Robert Wroth*. It includes poems by sons of Ben—Thomas Carew's *To Saxham* and *To my friend G. N. from Wrest,* Herrick's *A country-life: to his brother Mr Thomas Herrick* and *A panegyric to Sir Lewis Pemberton*—and pretty well the last of the line is Marvell's *Upon Appleton House*; except for a collateral descent through the topographical genre (Denham's *Cooper's Hill*; Pope's *Windsor Forest*).[3] Fittingly, Jonson's seminal exemplar was challenged by a great centre of patronage. For Penshurst's lord was Robert Sidney, Lord Lisle, who belonged to a family of brilliant literary patrons. We have to imagine the place as equally prominent on the map of letters with any college. As Patricia Thomson remarks, 'the strength of the Sidneys and Herberts as patrons lay in a form of enlightened hospitality'.[4]

Embattled Houses.

To Penshurst, like much of Jonson's poetry, makes many readers aware of a special relation of ideal with real. The two seem already embattled in the initial opposition between an idealized Penshurst and a sort of Timon's villa: between the reverenced 'ancient pile' and ambitious houses built as show places. But Penshurst was quite a modest

[3] Molesworth 155–6 distinguishes the two genres (country-house poems, e.g., have no court–country polarity); but with difficulty. Even *To Sir Robert Wroth* is a hybrid, verging on praise of retirement. On the taxonomic problem see J. W. Foster, *JEGP* 69 (1970) 394–406. R. Williams *The Country and the City* (1973) 26 ff. confuses the country-house poem with pastoral and ideology, but makes interesting and serious comments. On Pope's imitation of *To Penshurst* see M. Mack *The Garden and the City* (Toronto, etc. 1969) Index s.v. *Jonson*. Consult also J. Chalker *The English Georgic* (1969).

[4] Art. cit. above n. 1, pp. 275–6. Sir Philip Sidney, his sister Mary Ctess of Pembroke, his d. Elizabeth Ctess of Rutland (according to Jonson 'nothing inferior to her father in poetry'), his niece Lady Mary Wroth and his nephew Wm Herbert 3rd E. of Pembroke were all both patrons and writers. Sir Robt Sidney himself (Philip's brother), Visc. Lisle from 1605, was Chamberlain of the Queen's household, involved in organizing court masques.

(Cambridge 1973) 17 argues that the country-house poem reflects a modern way of life and lacks Latin analogues; while P. M. Cubeta, *PQ* 42 (1963), discusses the ancient sources. Renaissance antecedents include river encomia by Leland (1545), Camden (1586), Vallans (1590) and Spenser (1595). Jonson addresses Camden—'to whom I owe/ All that I am in arts'— in *Epig.* 14.

building in historical fact, with a fourteenth-century hall unimpressive
by Elizabethan standards. Far from being designed for 'show' it was
scarcely architect-designed at all; having grown by accretion into a
traditional, irregular, functional form.[5] By contrast, the pretentious
palaces which Sir John Summerson has termed 'prodigy houses' were
status symbols never meant for continuous occupation, but only for
reception of the court during the sovereign's progresses: 'Sir Francis
Willoughby built Wollaton purely and simply as an extravaganza';
'Hatton hardly used his new house [Holdenby], nor did he build it
for use'.[6] Designed for spectacular display and characterized by a conspicuously ostentatious extravagance that sometimes issued in quite
astonishing vulgarity, these competitive palaces—

> prouder piles, where the vain builder spent
> More cost in outward gay embellishment
> Than real use[7]

as Carew says—were indeed 'built to envious show'. Burghley, for
example, was criticized for building beyond his means or necessity,
and in a letter of 1585 he deprecates the riches of a stateroom at
Theobalds quite defensively. Its magnificence (which appears to have
run to imitation trees and an indoor waterfall) was exaggerated, he
writes; it 'need not be envied'.[8]

Jonson's negative statements—'Thou art not' this, 'nor canst
boast' that; 'Thou hast no lantern, whereof tales are told'—imply
real alternative possibilities. Herford and the Simpsons comment
with tedious brevity: 'There is a louvre at Penshurst Place, but
Jonson's point, which we do not follow, appears to be that it has no

---

[5] On the type, see Sir J. Summerson *Architecture in Britain 1530 to 1830*
(Harmondsworth 1953) 62–3, and J. Newman *West Kent and the Weald*
(Harmondsworth 1969) 438–9; A. M. Everitt *The Community of Kent and the
Great Rebellion 1640–60* (Leicester 1966), emphasizes Kentish use of local
materials, e.g. Penshurst's sandstone and ragstone. A vivid picture of great
house life emerges from Everitt: see esp. ch. 2 and Index s.v. *Penshurst* and
Penshurst Place. 'Pile' meant a *small* castle, a peel (*OED* s.v. *Pile* sb.²);
Burghley at first meant Theobalds 'for a little pile'—Peck *Desiderata curiosa*
(1598) cit. J. Nichols *Progresses . . . of Q. Elizabeth* 3 vols (1823) 1.309 n.
[6] Cit. Summerson *Architecture in Britain* 30–3, 41; cf. H. A. Tipping *English
Homes* Period 3, vol. 2 *Late Tudor and Early Stuart* (1927) and Hibbard 160.
Id. 161 writes of the declining importance of the hall in the 17th cent.;
but the houses of prodigy Jonson meant were earlier in design.
[7] T. Carew *To my friend G. N. from Wrest* 53–5; ed. R. Dunlap (Oxford
1949) 87.
[8] V.C.H. *Herts.* 3.448; Nichols *Progresses . . . of Q. Elizabeth* 1.205.

special history'. And John Carey has ingeniously discovered an allusion to Theobalds, over which a belfry lantern with a chiming clock and dials showing the zodiac and planets was prominent.[9] Now, Jonson certainly had hard things to say in private about the Earl of Salisbury, Burghley's second son and owner of Theobalds until 1607. But he would scarcely have risked publishing such a slight unless it was at least concealed among the ambages of possible allusions to other palaces. And in fact the Theobalds lantern belonged to a tradition: the same tradition with the Hampton Court hall louvre and the Nonesuch clock tower.[10] As for the Earl of Shrewsbury's Worksop (before 1590), it sported no less than four prominent lanterns on corner towers.

Other architectural features in the opening lines are similarly characteristic of contemporary houses in the grand style. 'Stair' is particularly suggestive: Burghley had a magnificent stone-vaulted stair; and Knole in Kent, where Lord Treasurer Sackville around 1605 built staterooms of exceeding sumptuousness, could boast the first English staircase treated as an architectural spectacle (but one soon imitated at Hatfield, Blickling and Aston Hall).[11] As to 'courts', Kirby and Burghley had one each, Theobalds and Holdenby two, and Knole seven, possibly in accordance with a temporal symbolism. The court plan was designed to provide lodgings or suites for large-scale, and sometimes big-businesslike, entertaining such as was beyond the means of Lord Lisle.[12] Again, 'touch', black granite or marble, was common, for example in the portentous mantelpieces then fashionable.[13] At Wrest Park, writes Carew, 'No sumptuous chimney piece of shining stone . . . coldly entertains' the visitor's sight.[14]

That a moral antitype, rather than a lampoon of Salisbury, is in-

---

[9] Private communication. According to a 17th-cent. Parliamentary Survey, the Theobalds lantern was 'of excellent workmanship curiously wrought standing a great height with divers pinnacles at each corner'. See Sir J. Summerson 'The Building of Theobalds, 1564–1585' *Archaeologia* 97 (1959) 107–26; I. Dunlop *Palaces and Progresses of Elizabeth I* (1962) 175. Other features include a notable dogleg stair (Summerson 'Theobalds' 122) and a fountain of white and black marble or 'touch' (ibid. 119; V.C.H. *Herts.* 3.250).   [10] Summerson 'Theobalds' 118.
[11] Newman 81, 347; Summerson *Architecture in Britain* 39, 53. J. C. A. Rathmell, *ELR* 1 (1971) 256, identifies Knole as Jonson's main target.
[12] Summerson *Architecture in Britain* 34. On Lisle's straitened means see Rathmell *passim*.   [13] Newman 345, 347–8.
[14] *To my friend G. N.* 25–7; ed. Dunlap 87.

tended finds support in Gayle Wilson's discovery of Biblical allusions. The idolatrous Solomon's Temple in *1 Kings* 6-7[15] had prominent 'pillars of brass', 'winding stairs', an 'inner court' and a 'great court', besides being 'overlaid with gold'.[16] Wilson's argument is not un-assailable: *lights* were windows, not lanterns. But Solomon's profane temple may well form a wing of the anti-palace. If so, it is curious that an entertainment of Jonson's, performed at Theobalds in 1606 for the visit of King James with the king of Denmark, contained a repre-sentation of Solomon's Temple.[17]

Besides prodigy houses and the Biblical type of Solomon's Temple, this densely allusive passage may also glance at the pagan archi-tectural wonders that Milton quarried for his Pandemonium and Spenser for his Panthea—the Pantheon, Holovitreum and Capitol of the medieval *Mirabilia urbis Romae*.[18] The stately Capitol, used in Du Bellay's *Vision* as a symbol of Rome, in some sense resembled a lantern, for it had a wall of 'shining crystal'. And its roof was of gold:

> Gold was the parget and the ceiling bright
> Did shine all scaly with great plates of gold.[19]

With such types belong Spenser's proud House of Lucifera, with its 'golden foil' and 'dial', as well as the houses Jonson contrasts with Durrants, 'free from proud porches, or their gilded roofs'.[20] But then, so does Spenser's good Panthea, about which tales are quite literally told.[21] Besides setting up an evil antitype, Jonson may also be refer-ring to royal palaces, in comparison with which Penshurst quite properly falls short. Theobalds, on the other hand, was so ambitious a heap that in 1607 James I exchanged Hatfield for it, at a ceremony for which Jonson himself wrote a masque.

[15] G. E. Wilson, *SEL* 8 (Houston, Texas 1968) 79–81, 84, and 88, comparing Vaughan *The Shepherds* 17–26.
[16] cf. *1 Kings* 7.6, 15–22; 6.8; 6.36; 7.9, 12; 6.22.
[17] Letter from Sir J. Harington cit. Nichols *Progresses . . . of K. James* 4 vols (1828) 2.72, alleging that James became very drunk, and that the performance so far deteriorated that the Q. of Sheba tripped, emptying her gifts into the Danish king's lap.
[18] For this 12th-cent. guide-book, see M. R. Scherer *Marvels of Ancient Rome* (New York and London 1955) 4 *et passim*; also Rathborne 25.
[19] *Visions* 2, Variorum *Minor Poems* 2.179; cf. *Theatre* 2, ibid. 2.12. *Parget*: ornamental plasterwork.
[20] *F.Q.*1.4.4; *To Wroth* 14, ed. Herford and Simpson 8.97.
[21] On *Mirabilia* materials used for Panthea (*F.Q.*1.10.58, 2.10.73) see Rathborne 25 ff.; ibid. 67 rejects Warton's suggestion of Windsor as model.

Cosmic Symbolism at Penshurst.

The architectural passage has a central bearing on the form of the poem. A characteristic feature of prodigy houses was their elaborate planning: meant as impressive spectacles, they were often carefully proportioned, with an ideal form objectifying some political or philosophical idea. Theobalds, besides the great chamber's zodiac ceiling, had twelve bells and a zodiac in its lantern recalling the Holovitreum 'made of glass and gold by mathematical craft, where was an astronomy with all the signs of heaven'.[22] Knole reckoned 365 rooms, 52 staircases, and 7 courts. And Thorpe's design for Longford Castle (1580) developed an extravagant trinitarian conceit. Indeed, a broad category of houses with programmatic designs can be distinguished.[23] But Penshurst, a house that had developed through the accretions of centuries, could offer no such ideal significances. Nor had Lord Lisle the financial resources to do much to follow the fashion, however much he might wish to.[24] That is why Jonson credits Penshurst instead with 'better marks', or symbols of another sort.[25] These he finds in its estate: most of the poem goes to show that Penshurst is dignified by as much order and symbolism as the prodigy houses, but in land and use rather than architectural display:

> they that will proportion thee
> With other edifices, when they see
> Those proud ambitious heaps, and nothing else,
> May say, their lords have built, but thy lord dwells.

The 'better marks' of Penshurst include 'marks, of soil, of air,/Of wood, of water'. Here the ideal is microcosmic significance: Penshurst may lack something of the elements of architecture, but it has the four cosmic elements in good proportion. The fourth, fire, resides potentially in the 'wood' used to make it, an association repeated in the 'writhed bark' of Sidney's Oak, which records the silvans 'taken with his flames'.[26] Such tropic flames of love, zeal and hospitality

[22] ibid. 26.

[23] Summerson *Architecture in Britain* 41–2. Chilham in Kent had a geometrical symbolism: see M. Girouard *Robert Smythson and the Architecture of the Elizabethan Era* (S. Brunswick and New York n.d.) 39 'Architecture and the Device'.   [24] On Lisle's wish to enlarge his park see Rathmell 258.

[25] *OED* s.v. *Mark* sb. III 10.

[26] Lines 15–16: either 'his passion' or 'the same passion as Sidney's'; cf. Waller *At Penshurst* 3, 13–14; ed. G. T. Drury 1 (1893) 64–5: 'When to the beeches I report my flame', 'all we can of love or high desire,/ Seems but the smoke of amorous Sidney's fire'.

flicker over Penshurst like a benign St Elmo's fire: fire warms the visiting poet's room without his asking, and fires of hospitality

>Shine bright on every hearth, as the desires
>Of thy Penates had been set on flame
>   (ll. 78–9)

—inviting the king to pay an impromptu visit. In its broadest application, fire symbolizes the warmth of the country's loyalty (80–1). The other elements also reappear: the Medway and the fishpond with their produce (22, 31–8), the 'lower land' and 'middle grounds' with theirs (22–30), and the 'fresh . . . air' (40). In this, as in much else, Carew's *To Saxham* follows *To Penshurst*; though with a simpler manner:

>Water, earth, air, did all conspire,
>To pay their tributes to thy fire.[27]

Carew, too, distributes produce between the elements and gives honour of place to hospitable fire, highest of the elements.

Like Ausonius in *De Mosella*, Jonson turns from marble splendours to discover Nature's artistry more harmonious, intricate, consummate and compressed than any human imitation.[28] His inventory of Penshurst estate gives a strong sense of order as well as abundant plentitude. Yet this effect is oddly unaccountable. Though he mentions many items, it is to catalogue rather than describe or realize them. There is little sensuous particularity: even 'the painted partridge' functions less as an image than as an allusion, through Martial's *picta perdix*, to Faustinus' homely farm.[29] How, then, is the effect of fertile plenty sustained? A clue may lie in the labyrinthine elaboration of Jonson's arrangement of items in relation to one another. The effects of Penshurst form highly ordered sets, and it may partly be these that communicate impressions of inexhaustible complexity and completeness.[30] Well might Oldham say 'No shuffled atoms did the well-built work compose'. Not only has Jonson ordered the poem's substantive catalogues and formal divisions, but he has ordered them

[27] Lines 29–30, ed. Dunlap 28; cf. *To my friend G.N.* 25–8, ibid. 87: 'No sumptuous chimney-piece . . . but clear/ And cheerful flames'.
[28] *De Mosella* 48–52: 'Now go, and with Phrygian slabs lay smooth floors spreading an expanse of marble through your fretted halls. But I, despising what wealth and riches have conferred, will marvel at Nature's handiwork, not at the ruin of prodigals, at reckless extravagance'.
[29] *Epig.* 3.58.15.
[30] See L. Beaurline, *PMLA* 84 (1969) 51–9, for a perceptive study of structural completeness in Jonson's drama.

according to several independent organizational ideas, which we may now review.

Spatial and Temporal Arrangement.

First the topography is divided into distinct, exhaustively enumerated levels, through which the reader passes on separate 'walks' (9): 'Mount'; 'middle grounds'; 'lower land'; 'river'; 'banks'; 'tops'. One formal division has also a spatial plan: as Paul Cubeta has noted the poem's first half treats the exterior of the house, the second half the interior. The transition is at line 48, where 'all come in, the farmer, and the clown'. Outdoors the estate's teeming provision, indoors the cornucopias of tribute and hospitality and the inner magnificence of noble or spiritual fruitfulness.[31]

Secondly, there are temporal arrangements. Fruits are not only set in the flowering branches of harmoniously balanced pre-Augustan rhetoric, but come in seasonal schemes:

Then hath thy orchard fruit, thy garden flowers,
Fresh as the air, and new as are the hours.
The early cherry, with the later plum,
Fig, grape, and quince, each in his time doth come:
The blushing apricot, and woolly peach
Hang on thy walls, that every child may reach.[32]

The catalogue divides 2 | 3 | 2, comprising 2 temporal opposites 'early . . . later'; 3 'each in his time'; and 2 more temporal opposites (*apricot* meaning early-ripe, before other peaches), moderated by the coy blushing of the precocious ripener. The 3 fruiting times realize the 'new . . . hours', that is, *Horae*, the divinities presiding over the seasons of the ancient year. Other items similarly represent stages of growth succeeding in the fullness of time. 'Mares, and horses breed'; kine have calves; and 'bright (i.e., mature) eels', 'fat, aged carps', 'ripe daughters' and the 'fruitful' lady are all creatures who, in Spenser's words, 'by their change their being do dilate', working their perfection.[33] The natural achieves here an ideal season

[31] See Cubeta 17. The most obvious sections are: lines 1–6 architecture | 7–8 elements | 9–48 provisions: outdoors | 49–88 hospitality: indoors | 89–98 virtues | 99–102 architecture. Or, *6 | 2 | 40 | 40 | 10 | 4.*
In *To Wroth* the outdoors-indoors division is a simple bisection.
[32] Lines 39–44; see Cubeta 21 and (on Lisle's interest in fruit-growing) Rathmell 252–3.
[33] *F.Q.*.7.7.58; see Wilson 81. J. Hart 'Ben Jonson's Good Society' *Modern Age* 7 (1962–3) cit. Gill 228 discusses Penshurst as an ideal organic community.

of fruition and oblation. Jonson's poem is as Christian as the patron himself and his country-house society; yet the generic economy of communication assumes ancient landscape types which go back to the feasting Golden Age of Hesiod's *Works and Days*, with its fertile earth bearing fruit in abundance, and of *Odyssey* 7, the inexhaustible garden of Alcinous.[34]

Temporal order also appears in broader sequences. The largest sequence begins with Lisle's 'ancient' inheritance from the past, his estate, and moves through its present enjoyment and use in hospitality and loyal service to provision for the future by the nurture of children. This scheme corresponding to the three parts of time provides Penshurst with the historical setting, which Charles Molesworth claims to be an essential *differentia* of the country-house poem (pp. 142–3). The time-span implied is longer than an individual life. Thus the legacy of the past includes

that taller tree, which of a nut was set,
    At his great birth, where all the Muses met

—that is, the Bear's Oak (so called after the badge of the Dudleys), said to have been planted at the birth of Sir Philip Sidney, Robert's elder brother.[35] It is a family tree, commemorating a heritage of greatness, a tradition of patronage. As Molesworth puts it, the country-house poem engages the 'life of memory', arousing a sense of the patron's virtuous forefathers.[36] More remotely, the oak's roots reach down, through mythology of feasting gods (10–12), to an earthly paradise of accessible fruit; to the golden age; to a cosmic past. But Jonson also availed himself of an English landscape type, generated by Leland's *Cygnea cantio*, in which every house was clothed in an ivy of encomiastic historical allusion.

The present is time to spend and enjoy, so that the poem's second part treats Penshurst's hospitality. Lisle's warm and 'liberal' (but not extravagant) hospitality is contrasted with the mingy parsimony of a disagreeable new sort of 'great man'. These might be ostentatious in entertaining V.I.P.s, but doled out their hospitality to others grudgingly, with a close eye on expense. Jonson's praise of 'high huswifery' at Penshurst gains historical perspective from his mingled complaint about the contemporary decline ('this day') in a

---

[34] Hesiod *Works and Days* 110–20. On the landscape type see H. M. Richmond *Renaissance Landscapes* (The Hague 1973) 25 *et passim*.
[35] See Herford and Simpson 11.33.
[36] Jonson's phrase: see Molesworth 144.

traditional liberality of 'housekeeping' that had formerly made the great house an important cell of social organization. Like many observers, Jonson deplored the tendency away from informal direct dealings towards contractuality, commercial system and impersonal bureaucratic administration. It was a period that saw 'household economy put on a business footing'.[37] Against this system, against 'this age' (l.92) of historically deteriorating manners, Jonson sets the ideal feast, the national golden age, still lingering, still celebrated, perpetuated in reality, at Penshurst.

The third part of time is approached in the concluding passage, through the upbringing of the new generation in 'manners, arms, and arts' by the example of their 'virtuous parents' (97–8). Penshurst's true estate, the 'fruit' (90) and 'fortune' (92) of human values that he will leave to posterity, dwells in these children. To this explicitly Christian hope—the children 'are, and have been taught religion'— Jonson leads up through a passage of implicit eschatology. King James's unexpected visit conforms to Biblical types of the coming of the kingdom, when men, like stewards and brides, are judged by their readiness for the master's sudden arrival.[38]

Hierarchical Order.

Another organizing principle is the hierarchical, early at work in the catalogue of trees, where 'that taller tree' is the primate, oak (Bear's Oak, Lady's Oak). Critics have taken several hints at the Great Chain of Being, in which the duty of the lower orders was to serve man. A chief end of the encomium, as in later country-house poems, is to dignify the patron by showing that creatures on his estate enjoy fulfilling their subservient roles. An unusually virtuous lord influences wild life to an unusually willing, even enthusiastic, sacrifice. At Penshurst the copse 'never fails to serve . . . deer', 'each bank doth yield' rabbits, the partridge 'is willing to be killed', pikes 'themselves betray', eels 'leap on land / Before the fisher, or into his hand' and the apricot and peach so hang 'that every child may reach'. Critics have aptly cited *Genesis* 9, where God, commanding fruitful-

---

[37] R. H. Tawney 'The Rise of the Gentry, 1558–1640' *Econ. Hist. Rev.* 11 (1941) 5, 10, 33–8; Molesworth 147–50; Hibbard 159, 161. Camden noticed 'the decay of the glory of hospitality' together with a 'riot of banqueting': see Black 267.

[38] e.g. *Mark* 13.32–7; see Wilson 86. With the bright fires that attract the king, perhaps cf. the lamps of *Matt.* 25.

ness, gives man (in the person of Noah) dominion over other creatures: '*into your hand* are they delivered'.[39] Yet Wilson and Hibbard (p. 164) may be wrong to take the partridge's submission entirely at face value. 'Willing to be killed' surely recalls the 'ipse capi voluit' of Juvenal's turbot (*Sat.* 4.69), in a context of 'gross flattery'. May not Jonson intend that playful panegyric tone which depends on openly hyperbolic excess of flattery?

The political links of the Great Chain appear more obviously in an ascending series of visitors: neighbours with their tribute of unnecessary gifts (ll. 49–60), the guest (61–2), the poet favoured with service fit for the king or lord (74) and finally the king himself, to whom the Sidneys offered tribute of hospitality and from whom they 'reaped' in turn a harvest of praise. Characteristically, Jonson makes this series of stewardship relations lead up to a sudden enlargement into eschatology: the royal test of the house's readiness is a symbol of God's judgement of man. As Lisle holds Penshurst in fee from James, so James is a steward too, responsible for his kingdom to the divine lord, whose coming he expects.[40]

King James comes last and greatest of all the visitors, at the place of honour in ancient triumphal processions. But he may also be dignified numerologically, by the formal position of his name and first introduction 27 lines from the end, matching a mention of 'crown' ('To crown thy open table') 27 lines from the beginning. The number 27, the cube of the number of limitation, was sacred to Cybele, goddess of the natural law that landlords must obey; and Cybele's familiar attribute was a crown.[41]

Numerological Design.

Lester Beaurline contrasts Jonson's completeness of treatment with an 'older more simply quantitative' copiousness through numerical

---

[39] *Gen.* 9.2. Carew *To Saxham* 21–8, modelled on Jonson, makes the allusion to Noah explicit (Wilson 82–3).

[40] See Cubeta 18, 22; Wilson 85–6; Rivers 41. R. Williams finds the hierarchic theme unpalatable: Penshurst is a paradise of 'easy consumption', from which the curse of labour is extracted 'by a simple abstraction of the existence of labourers' (32). But are waiters and cheese-makers abstracted?

[41] Cartari 112. According to Boccaccio, the crown is Earth's circlet, set with cities, castles and villages. Cubeta 19 notices the pun. On a similar use of 27 to symbolize Cybele see Fowler *Numbers of Time* 186.

schemes (p. 55). But the seventeenth-century poet's structural style seems to me no less numerological than that of his predecessors, although its indicators may be more subtly internalized.

We notice that the 17 creatures yielding 'free provisions' (i.e. stock) fall into three groups: animals or birds (creatures of the various 'grounds'); fish; and fruit (produce of the orchard). The items are arranged as symmetrically as any palace façade—*deer* | *sheep* | *cows* | *horses* | *conies* | *pheasant* | *partridge* | | *carp* | *pike* | *eel* | | *cherry* | *plum* | *fig* | *grape* | *quince* | *apricot* | *peach*, or 7 | 3 | 7. Possibly the heptads are to be subdivided. The motif of 7 as the union of 4 and 3 was a common number symbol, signifying the power of the creative *tetraktus* to form the cosmic heptad from the limiting triad and the elemental tetrad. Alternatively, it referred to the sevenfold grace of the Trinity's triad and the Gospel's tetrad.[42] Penshurst's 7 land creatures comprise 4 domestic and 3 wild species; just as the orchard, as we saw, yields (2 + 3 + 2) fruits. Similarly, the neighbours' 7 gifts are capons, cake, nuts, apples, together with 3 from the cheese producers (cheese itself, pears, plums).[43] More obviously, many of the groupings are simple triads: trees (beech, chestnut, oak), mythological beings on the mount (dryads, satyrs, fauns), copses (Gamage's, Ashore, Sidney's), comforts ('fire, or lights, or livery'). Latterly, the triads become more abstract: Lady Lisle is 'noble, fruitful, chaste'; the children learn mysteries of 'manners, arms and arts'.

The external form is also numerically organized. A division between outdoors and indoors draws some attention to the midpoint, where encomiums commonly introduced some prominent mention of the person honoured. Here, Penshurst's 'lord, and lady' are first mentioned in the fiftieth of 102 lines.

That Jonson should make *To Penshurst* in 51 couplets, rather than the round-number 50 or the calendrical 52 would not have seemed puzzling to his first readers. For 51 was a common compositional number, from its structural use in the *Psalms*. Pietro Bongo, least original of Renaissance arithmologists, explains it as the product of 3 and 17, the latter symbolizing the Decalogue together with the sevenfold gifts of the Spirit. He further associates 17 with St John's miraculous draught of 153 fish (or species of fish), since that symbol of the

---

[42] Bongo 197, 287. Pico expatiates on the threefold and fourfold universe in the authoritative *Heptaplus*, 2nd Proem; tr. D. Carmichael, ed. P. J. W. Miller (New York 1965) 78–9.
[43] On precedents for numerology of gifts, see Fowler *Triumphal Forms* 64.

Elect was analysed as the triangular number on 17 as base.[44] Now Jonson, as we saw, has 17 species provisioning Penshurst estate (with the fish, incidentally, forming a prominent central group). Is it possible that the 51 couplets of the poem itself are divided into thirds of 17 couplets each? Sure enough, a division between the first two thirds is wittily noticed in the lines on either side:

> pikes, now weary their own kind to eat,
>> As loth, the second draught, or cast to stay,
>> Officiously, at first, themselves betray.

Draught, primarily the drawing of a net (*OED* III 7), means also a passage of writing (*OED* XII 38). Thus the pikes are too eager to wait for Part 2, but press forward into the seventeenth couplet and Part 1; so that their dutifulness puts them in the sovereign central place of 17 species.[45] The solemn view that the fishes' willing sacrifice expresses creaturely acceptance of the Chain of Being is no doubt right, but it hardly does justice to the wit of Jonson's Biblical allusions.

The third draught, beginning at line 69, is again signalled by a reference to counting: 'Here no man tells (counts) my cups'. An inhospitable great man's waiter stands just at the division, to count draughts in another sense, the thirsty poet's drinks, ordered in the first line of Part 3.

If this were all, *draught* would already be a complex word. But the prominence of architectural symbolism makes a third pun on *draught* not impossible. It could mean 'a measure of sawyers' work' in stonemasonry: a use that would come naturally to Jonson, a former mason.[46] The poetic collation he adds to the Sidneys' feast may be edifying in far more senses than his plain style has led us to think.

If we distinguish an architectural introduction of 3 couplets, contrasting Penshurst with prodigy houses, and an architectural coda of

---

[44] ibid. 189 citing Bongo 594–5 on *John* 21.11. According to Gregory the Great and others, 17 means the Decalogue together with the 7-fold Spirit. Multiplied by the divine triad, 17 yields first 51, then 153. The miraculous draught was much discussed in the Renaissance: see J. Shearman
Raphael's Cartoons in the Collection of Her Majesty the Queen and the Tapestries for the Sistine Chapel (1972).
[45] On symbolism of the centre see Fowler *Triumphal Forms* chs. 2–5.
E. McCutcheon 'Jonson's *To Penshurst*, 36' *Expl.* 25 (1967) Item 52 catches a pun in 'officiously'.
[46] *OED* s.v. *Draught* IV 12. Solomon's 3-chambered temple called for 'measures of hewed stones': *1 Kings* 6.6, 7.9–11 (illus. in Geneva vers.).

2 couplets, the 51 couplets also divide 3 | 46 | 2. Traditionally 46 meant 'edification', the building of a regenerate human nature as a temple of the spirit (the association was with the second Temple of Jerusalem which took 46 years to build).[47] Moreover, the 10 framing lines symbolize the *tetraktus* of virtue that informs Penshurst. Perhaps we are to see the substantive architecture of introduction and coda as the setting for architecture composed in a more organic manner. At least the affirmation 'their lords have built, but thy lord dwells' has acquired a remarkable resonance. The other 'edifices' are built with hands and owned by absentee landlords who reside only as occasional ostentatious hosts; but Penshurst is the creaturely temple of a regenerate spirit who dwells in the house of the Lord and who, though often absent physically, even as host, is spiritually present in his estate, perpetually hospitable, imaging the divine Lord who dwells in his universe. Hence the *prosopopeia* to Penshurst estate simultaneously addresses Penshurst the man. To 'proportion' it (99) means not merely compare, but shape and divide in the fair proportions of Lisle's nature.[48]

Moral Order and Degree.

The moral character of the well-ordered estate is displayed both in direct examples and in emblems. Already in the Latin poets the form of an estate could express character: Ausonius could write 'But you must know what size this estate of mine is, so that you may know me —and know yourself too if you are capable'. And after Jonson, as Molesworth remarks, country-house poem estates were regularly to 'reflect the virtue and character of the owner' by metonymy.[49] From this point of view it is a brilliant stroke to delay the entry of the Sidneys, so that until the sudden salute at the poem's centre we learn of them only obliquely, through their property.

Not that Lisle's 'creatures' and household all appear in an ideal light. A lordly supercharacter, it seems, may generate not only good

[47] The symbolism also depends on the numerical value of *Adam* (Bongo 527–31). For literary examples see Fowler *Numbers of Time* 54. Spirit as an informing *tetraktus* is discussed ibid. 275 ff.
[48] See *OED* s.v. *Proportion* vb, 2, 4. Rathmell 252 documents Lisle's frequent absences on official business.
[49] Ausonius *Opusc.* 3.1.17–18 cit. Richmond 37; Molesworth 145. Prosperity was now one of 'the plainest signs' of God's blessing (Q. Elizabeth's Letter to the D. of Florence).

but also vicious subcharacters. Here virtue shows up against foils of ambitious social climbing, which range in culpability from the emulous eel (an overreacher who leaves his true element to leap on land) and the Medway (too 'high-swollen'[50] sometimes to pay its tribute), through tolerantly-observed neighbours vying to marry their daughters well,[51] to the degree-conscious 'great man' satirized for inhospitality, who denied Jonson the status accorded him by Lisle.[52] Even the thirsty poet is presented critically, as an image of excess, an extreme opposite to businesslike niggardliness: Sir Toby to the waiter's Malvolio, Sansloy to the bad host's Elissa. As true mean there stands the liberal moderation of Lisle, a 'taller tree' between ambitious Pan and lawless Bacchus. The Lisles' 'freedom doth with degree dispense',[53] so that they can treat the poet as if he 'reigned', while fully acknowledging their duty to the real king. True hospitality being a free and reciprocal communion, Wilson (p. 85) can intelligibly find a symbol of the Lord's Supper in 'thy lord's own meat . . . and bread, and self-same wine' (ll. 62–3).

Jonson explicitly announces the emblematic mode where it is least obvious, in the gifts of the 'ripe daughters'

whose baskets bear

An emblem of themselves in plum, or pear.

By so doing, he draws attention beyond the prominent sensuousness,

---

[50] Cubeta 19 finds in 'high-swollen Medway' a 'suggestion of luxuriant . . . abundance'. But the word was morally dyslogistic, implying excess: see *OED* s.v. *Swollen* 2 a, and cf. Milton *Samson* 532 'swollen with pride'. The Medway was hard to fish: see Rathmell 255.

[51] Not in Martial's description of the Baian villa. Cubeta's 'sly poking of fun at motives of calculating farmers' (22) is surer than Wilson's notion (84) of an allusion to Ruth.

[52] Eds. cite Jonson's *Conversations*, ed. Herford and Simpson 1.141, which purports to relate how he rebuked the E. of Salisbury: 'You promised I should dine with you, but I do not': he had none of the meat 'which was of his (i.e. Salisbury's) own dish'. Jonson's private opinion of Salisbury was critical on some occasions (cf. ibid. 1.142); but we should consider that the earl actually received praise for his hospitality (Nichols *Progresses . . . of K. James* 2.63), that Jonson's seemingly autobiographical verses echo epigrams of Martial's imitated also by others (*Epig.* 3.58.42–4; Herrick *A panegyric to Sir Lewis Pemberton* 45–70) and that Carew could *praise* a patron for making dietary discriminations (*To my friend G.N.* 37–42, ed. Dunlap 87: 'others of better note/ Whom wealth, parts, office, or the herald's coat/ Have severed from the common, freely sit/ At the lord's table').

[53] *To Wroth* 58; ed. Herford and Simpson 8.98.

beyond the rotundities held out by mature girls,[54] to the significance of their specific offerings. The pear was an emblem of accessibility ('The ripe pear falls even of its own freewill');[55] but the plum, as a 'later fruit' proverbial of difficulty ('The higher the plumtree the sweeter the plum'),[56] modifies the amenable suggestion.

Recommendatory panegyric

The last part of *To Penshurst* seems to present the Sidneian way of life more abstractly. But some of its generalization has been implicit already: the country-house poem views 'man's estate as the "effect" of his virtue'.[57] Lady Lisle 'reaps' praise and is 'fruitful', while her children read in their parents mysteries of manners earlier exemplified, or patronage symbolized by the tree lasting from 'his great birth, where all the Muses met'. The generalizations are idealistic, as the mode requires. But even in this section, specific facts are reflected: communal prayers were a feature of Kentish great house life.[58]

Each point of this kind (and many could be made) weakens Parfitt's objection that the poem gives no total impression of life at Penshurst, that 'the only hints of anything non-ideal are there for contrast'.[59] Indeed, it is remarkable how much of Penshurst can be found, once references are seen through the transformations of art. Parfitt concludes Jonson's achievement to be 'one of exclusion'. Oddly he finds the account of the hospitality 'clearly simplified'. But were the Sidneys not in actual fact remarkable patrons and hosts?

More plausibly, Hibbard contrasts Jonson, for whom Penshurst 'represents the norm, slightly idealized, perhaps, but still the norm', with Pope, for whom 'Timon's villa is the norm' (pp. 159–60). Certainly the later poet wrote differently, for a society much altered; but

---

[54] Growth stages of fruit—ripe or, like Ariosto's *pome acerbe*, unripe—were obvious metaphors for breast development: e.g. *Orl. Fur.* 7.14; Carew *A rapture* 66, ed. Dunlap 51.
[55] J. Cats *Proteus* (Rotterdam 1627) Embl. 11.1 MITE PYRUM VEL SPONTE FLUIT. For the pear as Venus' attribute, see Tervarent col. 309.
[56] Tilley P 441 citing J. Clarke *Paroemiologia anglo-latina* (1639) s.v. *Difficultatis*. For the plum = fidelity, see G. Ferguson *Signs and Symbols in Christian Art* (New York 1961) 37.
[57] Molesworth 145.
[58] Rathmell 254 cites an early 17th-cent. house rule which prescribed household prayers morning and evening; cf. Everitt 50 on Penshurst's influential piety under Henry Hammond.
[59] G. A. E. Parfitt 'The Poetry of Ben Jonson' *EC* 18 (1968) 29, uncritically accepted by Rivers (51).

the change hardly amounts to an absence of 'the values Pope believes in' from the great houses built in his time. It probably had more to do with the poets' attitudes to personal patronage. Pope, writing after the system had largely broken down, would be less interested in styles of patronage than in general moral qualities. But Jonson, addressing good patrons while the system still worked, would hope that specific portrayals of a noble life-style might have real influence.

To Penshurst, like other poems of its genre, unquestioningly accepts 'the social value of real property', at least when well used.[60] But its praise of Lisle's house never really strikes the 'somewhat offensive panegyric tone' which one critic has heard in it.[61] Indeed, its tone seems characterized by detached alertness. It reflects awareness of civilized forms achieved by society, and of the threat presented to them by excessive display. It observes, in fact, what has been called the crisis of the aristocracy, in the perversion of 'house-keeping', the decline of property as a mark of virtue, and the spread of monetary contractuality.[62] Moreover, far from being in a servile relation to his patron, Jonson takes for granted an easy friendship, if not an advisory responsibility. He may even be said to guide the aspirations of the ruling class by his encomiastic strategy.[63] Perhaps this is plainest when he writes on nurture with a hint of exhortation. But the full strategy only appears when it is known that Lisle was in somewhat straitened circumstances financially, yet at the same time sensitive enough about the modest size of his park to have contemplated enlargement.[64] Jonson's praise of Penshurst's better marks may have served as magnificently discreet advice reconciling Lisle to his existing estate. Throughout, true nobility is distinguished from mere lavishness, in measured praise: Penshurst welcomed King James promptly, not grandly: with '(great, I will not say, but) sudden cheer'. Jonson feels no need to cover up or avoid the facts. The Lisles' house was well ordered and always ready for genuine hospitality. For contrived splendours it had no need.

The Ideal, the Historical and the Real.

Nevertheless, as Parfitt says, the descriptions of *To Penshurst* are 'miniatures of Elizabethan ideals' in active detail. Only, the relation

---

[60] Molesworth 146; cf. 142, 145.   [61] Foster 396, 398.   [62] Molesworth 146–50.
[63] H. Maclean 'Ben Jonson's Poems: Notes on the Ordered Society' *Essays
. . . Presented to A.S.P. Woodhouse 1964* ed. M. MacLure and F.W. Watt
(Toronto 1964) 57; cf. Hibbard 159.   [64] Rathmell 255–6, 258.

between general ideals and real details is unusually intricate. It was also, doubtless, unusually conscious: Jonson held that a poet was responsible for having 'exact knowledge of all virtues, and their contraries; with ability to render the one loved, the other hated, by his proper embattling them'.[65] Cubeta has shown that while *To Penshurst* includes details of Faustinus' Baian villa, its ideal is radically different from Martial's. It combines the rude fertility of Faustinus' villa with an artificial 'patterned, formal beauty' much like the 'farm' of Bassus, rather than simply contrasting the two types.[66] The realistic details of the fertile country scene, themselves partly literary, form so many patterns and are informed with so much meaning that they overwhelm the reader with the rich, highly civilized art of Lisle's client, quite as much as with Nature's increase of his property.

Jonson interfuses art and nature, ideal and real in astonishing complexity. William V. Spanos ('The Real Toad in the Jonsonian Garden.[67]) notices his characteristic 'transfiguration of the real' by introducing classical mythology into the English estate:

> Thy Mount, to which the dryads do resort,
> Where Pan, and Bacchus their high feasts have made,
> Beneath the broad beech, and the chest-nut shade;
> That taller tree, which of a nut was set,
> At his great birth, where all the Muses met.
>   (ll. 10–14)

'The aesthetic pleasure', Spanos propounds, 'derives from the resonance generated by the fusion of the opposites'. However, Jonson's Penshurst is no vague *locus amoenus*, but a specific equivalent of the golden age. It is the same with *To Sir Robert Wroth*:

> Thus Pan, and Sylvane, having had their rites,
> Comus puts in, for new delights;
> And fills thy open hall with mirth, and cheer,
> As if in Saturn's reign it were.
>   (ll. 47–50)

Moreover, from the generalized neoclassical landscape of 'broad beech, and . . . chest-nut shade' with its mythological staffage there stands out one local detail: 'that taller tree' planted at Sir Philip Sidney's birth. At first this may seem natural detail in classical setting, a converse interplay of ideal and real also labelled by Spanos.

[65] *Discoveries*, ed. Herford and Simpson 8.595; cit. Cubeta 14.
[66] ibid. 16–17; see Hibbard 163, and cf. Martial *Epig.* 3.58.
[67] *JEGP* 68 (1969) 1–23.

But the reality is stranger. The passage alludes to another Martial epigram, in which a tree planted by Julius Caesar symbolizes his lasting memory and harmonious relation to the gods.[68] Thus Jonson opens a farther reach of idealization, this time literary and historical, associating Philip Sidney with the divine Caesar. Molesworth sees this simply as a reference to poetic genius—'Sidney, having conquered time by the enduring virtues of his poetry, assumes . . . his true mythological status' (p. 154). But I think Jonson intends a more serious and Christian deification.

Penshurst's alfresco feast of the gods continues with the hospitality indoors, adding yet another idealization. Jonson here assimilates the Banquet of Immortals type, commoner in the visual arts,[69] but by no means devoid of literary exemplars (Catullus' nuptial feast of Peneus and Thetis: Apuleius' marriage of Cupid and Psyche: Spenser's spousal feast for Thames and Medway). With this generic identification several features of *To Penshurst*, such as its images of plenty, are in full agreement.[70] Nor need we quite reject Wilson's interpretation of the feast as the Lord's Supper: it is a banquet of immortals too, the communion of saints of which Philip Sidney partakes. From these high suggestions the poet's extensive drinking of untold cups brings us noisily to earth. True, Jonson sometimes connected hard drinking with poetic inspiration, and 'when he was reconciled with the church and left off to be a recusant at his first communion in token of true reconciliation, he drank out all the full cup of wine'.[71] Still, we may feel that Bacchus finds in the poet a palpable avatar, and suffers by contrast with Sidney's godly feast.[72] The classical ideal, which formerly elevated the real, is now dwarfed by it: the mythological turns out through history to have foreshadowed the Christian.

The interaction of real and ideal that characterizes *To Penshurst* is in

[68] 9.61; cf. Cubeta 18.
[69] See E. Wind *Bellini's Feast of the Gods* (Cambridge, Mass. 1948); H. Bardon *Le festin des dieux* (Paris 1960).
[70] cf. Carew *To my friend G. N.* 57–60: 'Amalthea's horn/ Of plenty is not in effigy worn/ Without the gate, but she within the door/ Empties her free and unexhausted store.' Amalthea's abundant horn was a common feature of the divine feast type: see Ovid *Met.* 9.85–96. Also cf. the flocks in Catullus *Carm.* 64. [71] *Conversations* ed. Herford and Simpson 1.141.
[72] There may be a local allusion in lines 10–18; cf. Carew's imitation (n.70 above), praising the absence of statues, 'Ceres . . . in stone' and Bacchus 'on a marble tun'. Theobalds, e.g., boasted a Satyrs' walk and much statuary: see Summerson 'Theobalds' 116 n.1.

a word typological; so that Molesworth's frequent emphasis of the historical element, though it generates very interesting criticism, must itself, in the last resort, be judged unhistorical. Molesworth attributes to Jonson a post-Romantic neo-Kantian emergent ideal, much like that of Cassirer, whom he quotes at length. But Jonson's ideal was much less consciously historical. He was indeed concerned with '"lastingness", in terms of property, natural riches and personal virtue'.[73] But this may have seemed less a matter of historical tendencies than moral and spiritual choices. Virtue and vice were always embattled: there were good houses, bad houses, good stewards, bad stewards; and the difference was set eternally. Jonson awaited the coming of a kingdom which is always; just as the Sidneys prepared their children for a future which is not yet. If he moved towards something like a sense of historical responsibility, it may have been through exploring poetically the combination of ancient and Biblical types with modern topographical and antiquarian kinds invented by Leland and Camden.

To Penshurst is a more religious poem than most have taken it to be. But it is also intellectually more intricate. It conceals difficulty, however, by an easy style, to give a satisfying harmony of soft and hard. The poet manages such discretions so successfully that his style, or diction, has been called *plain* style. But it should be evident from the above that, in one poem at least, Jonson's style is plain in a manner fully compatible with rich allusion, delicate suggestion and complex wit. To arrive at these subtleties, a critic needs all the help he can get from generic features, which may well indeed be decisive for his interpretation. A reader who did not recognize the combination of triumphal with encomiastic motifs, of topographical with morally didactic kinds, or of psalmodic with classical forms would find much of *To Penshurst* plain and dull. Certainly he would miss the farther finesses whereby many of the generic features are edged into satiric sharpness.

[73] Molesworth 142.

Bibliography

List of editions cited more than once

A handful of pleasant delights. Ed. Hyder E.Rollins. New York 1965.

Alan of Lille (Alanus de Insulis). *The 'Anticlaudian' of Alain de Lille*. Tr. and ed. William Hafner Cornog. Philadelphia, Pa. 1935.

Allen, R.H. *Star Names: Their Lore and Meaning*. New York 1963.

Andreas Capellanus. *De amore libri tres*. Ed. E. Trojel. Munich 1964.

—*The Art of Courtly Love*. Tr. and ed. John Jay Parry. Records of Civilization Sources and Studies 33. New York 1941.

A Theatre for Spenserians. Ed. Judith M.Kennedy and James A.Reither. Toronto and Buffalo, N.Y. 1973.

Barlett, Phyllis B. *See* s.v. Chapman.

Beaurline, Lester. 'Ben Jonson and the Illusion of Completeness'. *PMLA* 84 (1969) 51–9.

Berger, Harry. 'Spenser's *Prothalamion*: an Interpretation'. *Essays in Criticism* 15 (1965) 363–80. Now in A. C.Hamilton (ed.) *Essential Articles for the Study of Edmund Spenser*. Hamden, Conn. 1972.

Black, J.B. *The Reign of Elizabeth 1558–1603*. Oxford History of England. Oxford 1959.

Boll, Franz. *Sphaera*. Leipzig 1903.

Bongo, Pietro. *Numerorum mysteria*. Bergamo 1591.

Boyd, John Douglas. 'Literary Interpretation and the *Subjective* Correlative: an Illustration from Wyatt'. *Essays in Criticism* 21 (1971) 327–46.

Brown, John Russell. *See* s.v. *Elizabethan Poetry*.

Buxton, John. *A Tradition of Poetry*. 1967.

Capellanus. *See* Andreas Capellanus.

Carew, Thomas. *The Poems of Thomas Carew with his Masque 'Coelum Britannicum'*. Ed. Rhodes Dunlap. Oxford 1949.

Cartari, Vicenzo. *Imagini delli dei de gl' antichi*. Venice 1647. Facs. ed. W.Koschatsky. Graz 1963.

Chapman, George. *The Poems of George Chapman*. Ed. Phyllis B.Bartlett. New York 1962.

Clements, Robert J. *Picta poesis*. Temi e testi 6. Rome 1960.

Conti, Natale. *Mythologiae*. Lyons 1653.

Cornog, William Hafner. *See* s.v. Alan of Lille.

Cowley, Abraham. *Poems*. Ed. A.R.Waller. Cambridge 1905.

Cubeta, Paul M. 'A Jonsonian Ideal: *To Penshurst*'. *Philological Quarterly* 42 (1963) 14–24.

Curtius, Ernst Robert. *European Literature and the Latin Middle Ages.*
Tr. Willard R. Trask. 1953.

Davis, Walter. *A Map of Arcadia: Sidney's Romance in Its Tradition.*
Yale Studies in English 158. New Haven, Conn. and London 1965.

Drayton, Michael. *The Works of Michael Drayton.* Ed. J.W. Hebel,
K. Tillotson and B.H. Newdigate. 5 vols. Oxford 1931–41.

Du Bartas [Guillaume de Salluste Sieur du Bartas]. *Divine weeks.*
Tr. Joshua Sylvester. 1613.

Duncan-Jones, Katherine. 'Sidney's Urania'. *Review of English Studies* n.s. 17
(1966) 123–32.

Dunlap, Rhodes. *See* s.v. Carew.

Elizabethan Poetry. Ed. John Russell Brown and Bernard Harris.
Stratford-Upon-Avon Studies 2. 1960.

Everitt, Alan M. *The Community of Kent and the Great Rebellion 1640–60.*
Leicester 1966.

Feuillerat, Albert. *See* Sidney, Sir Philip.

Foster, John Wilson. 'A Redefinition of Topographical Poetry'.
Journal of English and Germanic Philology 69 (1970) 394–406.

Fowler, Alastair D. S. *Spenser and the Numbers of Time.* 1964.
—*Triumphal Forms: Structural Patterns in Elizabethan Poetry.* Cambridge 1970.
—*See* s.v. *Silent Poetry.*

Friedman, Donald M. 'The Mind in the Poem: Wyatt's *They flee from me*'.
Studies in English Literature 1500–1900 7 (Houston, Texas 1967) 1–13.

Gerard, Albert S. 'Wyatt's *They flee from me*'. *Essays in Criticism* 11
(1961) 359–65.

Gill, Richard. *Happy Rural Seat: the English Country House and the Literary
Imagination.* New Haven, Conn. and London 1972.

Gombrich, E. H. *Symbolic Images: Studies in the Art of the Renaissance.*
London and New York 1972.

Greene, Richard Leighton. 'Wyatt's *They flee from me* and the Busily
Seeking Critics'. *Bucknell Review* 12. 3 (1964) 17–30.

Greenlaw, E. *See* s.v. Spenser, Edmund.

Hainsworth, J. D. 'Sir Thomas Wyatt's Use of the Love Convention'.
Essays in Criticism 7 (1957) 90–5.

Harris, Bernard. *See* s.v. *Elizabethan Poetry.*

Harvey, Gabriel. *Gabriel Harvey's Marginalia.* Ed. G. C. Moore Smith.
Stratford-Upon-Avon 1913.

Hebel, J. W. *See* s.v. Drayton, Michael.

Henkel, Arthur and Schöne, Albrecht (eds.). *Emblemata; Handbuch zur
Sinnbildkunst des XVI und XVII Jahrhunderts.* Stuttgart 1967.

Heraclitus. *See* s.v. Kirk, G. S.

Herford, Simpson and Simpson. *See* s.v. Jonson, Ben.

Hibbard, G. R. 'The Country-House Poem of the Seventeenth Century'.
Journal of the Warburg Institute 19 (1956) 159–74.

Hieatt, A. Kent. *Short Time's Endless Monument.* New York 1960.

Hirsch, Donald E., Jr. *Validity in Interpretation*. New Haven, Conn. 1967.

Hoskins, John. *Directions for speech and style*. Ed. Hoyt H. Hudson. Princeton, N.J. 1935.

Hunter, George K. 'Spenser's *Amoretti* and the English Sonnet Tradition'. In *A Theatre for Spenserians*. Ed. Judith M. Kennedy and James A. Reither. Toronto and Buffalo, N.Y. 1973. Pp. 124–44.

Jones, Emrys. *See* s.v. Surrey, Henry Howard, Earl of.

Jonson, Ben. *Ben Jonson*. Ed. C. H. Herford, Percy Simpson and Evelyn Simpson. 11 vols. Oxford 1925–52.

Kalstone, David. *Sidney's Poetry: Contexts and Interpretations*. Cambridge, Mass. 1965.

Keast, William R. *Seventeenth-Century English Poetry: Modern Essays in Criticism*. New York 1962.

Kennedy, Judith M. *See* s.v. *A Theatre for Spenserians*.

Kirk, G. S. *Heraclitus: The Cosmic Fragments*. Cambridge 1954.

Klibansky, Raymond; Panofsky, Erwin; and Saxl, Fritz. *Saturn and Melancholy: Studies in the History of Natural Philosophy Religion and Art*. 1964.

Lapp, John C. *See* s.v. Tyard, Pontus de.

Leishman, J. B. *Themes and Variations in Shakespeare's Sonnets*. Second edn. 1963.

Leland, John. κύκνειον ᾆσμα. *Cygnea cantio*. 1545.

Les blason anatomiques du corps féminin . . . composez par plusieurs poétes contemporains (1550). Ed. A. [van] B[ever]. Paris 1907.

Lever, J. W. *The Elizabethan Love Sonnet*. 1956.

Lewis, C. S. *English Literature in the Sixteenth Century Excluding Drama*. Oxford History of English Literature 3. Oxford 1954.

Macrobius. *Commentary on the Dream of Scipio*. Tr. W. H. Stahl. New York and London 1966.

Manilius. *Manilii astronomicon libri quinque*. Ed. Josephus Justus Scaliger and Julius Caesar Scaliger. Paris 1579.

Martz, Louis L. "The *Amoretti*: "Most Goodly Temperature" '. *Form and Convention in the Poetry of Edmund Spenser*. Ed. William Nelson. Sel. Papers from the English Inst. New York and London 1961.

Mason, H. A. *Editing Wyatt: an Examination of 'Collected Poems of Sir Thomas Wyatt'*. Cambridge 1972.

Mazzeo, Joseph A. 'A Critique of Some Modern Theories of Metaphysical Poetry'. *Modern Philology* 50 (1952) 88–96. Reptd in *Seventeenth-Century English Poetry: Modern Essays in Criticism*. Ed. William R. Keast. New York 1962. Pp. 63–74.

—*Renaissance and Seventeenth-Century Studies*. 1964.

Middleton, Christopher. *The history of heaven*. 1596.

Miller, David M. *The Net of Hephaestus: a Study of Modern Criticism and Metaphysical Metaphor*. De Proprietatibus Litterarum, Ser. Maior 11. The Hague and Paris 1971.

Miner, Earl. *The Metaphysical Mode from Donne to Cowley*. Princeton, N.J. 1969.

Molesworth, Charles. 'Property and Virtue: the Genre of the Country-House Poem in the Seventeenth Century'. *Genre* 1 (1968) 141–57.

Morris, Harry. 'Birds, Does and Manliness in *They flee from me*'. *Essays in Criticism* 10 (1960) 484–92.

Muir, Kenneth, and Thomson, Patricia (eds.). *Collected Poems of Sir Thomas Wyatt*. Liverpool 1969.

Nelson, C. E. 'A Note on Wyatt and Ovid'. *Modern Language Review* 58 (1963) 60–3.

Nelson, William (ed.). *Form and Convention in the Poetry of Edmund Spenser*. Sel. Papers from the English Inst. New York and London 1961.

Newman, John. *West Kent and the Weald*. The Buildings of England. Gen. ed. Nikolaus Pevsner. Harmondsworth 1953.

Nichols, John. *The Progresses and Public Processions of Queen Elizabeth*. New edn. 3 vols. 1823.

—*The Progresses, Processions, and Magnificent Festivities of King James the First*. 4 vols. 1828.

Norton, Dan S. 'Queen Elizabeth's "Bridal day"'. *Modern Language Quarterly* 5 (1944) 149–54.

—*The Background of Spenser's 'Prothalamion'*. Princeton Univ. Doct. Thesis P.685. 1940. 38.

Otis, Brooks. *Virgil: A study in Civilized Poetry*. Oxford 1964.

Oxford Dictionary of English Proverbs, The. Ed. F. P. Wilson. Third edn revd. Oxford 1970.

Panofsky, Erwin. *Renaissance and Renascences in Western Art*. 1960; reptd 1970.
—*See* s.v. Klibansky et al.

Parry, John Jay. *See* s.v. Andreas Capellanus.

Petrarca, Francesco. *Le Rime*. Ed. Giosuè Carducci, Severino Ferrari and Gianfranco Contini. Florence 1957.

Pontus de Tyard. *See* Tyard, Pontus de.

Praz, Mario. *Studies in Seventeenth-Century Imagery*. Sussidi Eruditi 16. Rome 1964.

Puttenham, George. *The art of English poesy*. Ed. Gladys D. Willcock and Alice Walker. Cambridge 1936.

Rathborne, Isabel E. *The Meaning of Spenser's Fairyland*. New York 1937.

Rathmell, J. C. A. 'Johnson, Lord Lisle, and Penshurst'. *English Literary Renaissance* 1 (1971) 250–60.

Reither, James A. *See* s.v. *A Theatre for Spenserians*.

Rendell, Vernon. *Wild Flowers in Literature*. 1934

Richmond, H. M. *Renaissance Landscapes: English Lyrics in a European Tradition*. De Proprietatibus Litterarum, Ser. Pract. 52. The Hague and Paris 1973.

Ringler, William A. *See* s.v. Sidney, Sir Philip.

Ripa, Cesare. *Iconologia*. Rome 1603.

—*Baroque and Rococo Pictorial Imagery: The 1758–60 Hertel Edition of Ripa's 'Iconologia' with 200 Engraved Illustrations*. Ed. Edward A. Maser. New York 1971.

Rivers, Isabel. *The Poetry of Conservatism 1600–1745: a Study of Poets and Public Affairs from Jonson to Pope*. Cambridge 1973.

Robertson, D. W. *A Preface to Chaucer.* Princeton, N.J. 1963.

Robertson, Jean. *See* s.v. Sidney, Sir Philip.

Rollins, Hyder E. *See* s.v. *A handful of pleasant delights.*

Ruthven, K. K. 'The Composite Mistress'. *Australian Universities Modern Language Association* 26 (1966) 198–214.

—*The Conceit.* The Critical Idiom 4 (1969).

Sacrobosco, Iohannes. *The 'Sphere' of Sacrobosco and Its Commentators.* Tr. and ed. Lynn Thorndike. Chicago 1949.

Saxl, Fritz. *See* s.v. Klibansky, Raymond et al.

Scaliger, Julius Caesar. *Poetices libri septem.* Lyons 1561. Facs. ed. August Buck. Stuttgart 1964.

Schöne, Albrecht. *See* s.v. Henkel, Arthur.

Sidney, Sir Philip. *The Poems of Sir Philip Sidney.* Ed. William A. Ringler. Oxford 1962.

—*The Prose Works of Sir Philip Sidney.* Ed. Albert Feuillerat. 4 vols. Cambridge 1912 reptd 1965.

—*The Countess of Pembroke's Arcadia (The Old Arcadia).* Ed. Jean Robertson. Oxford 1973.

Silent Poetry: Essays in Numerological Analysis. Ed. Alastair Fowler. 1970.

Smith, G. C. Moore. *See* s.v. Harvey, Gabriel.

Smith, J. Norton. 'Spenser's *Prothalamion:* a New Genre'. *Review of English Studies* n.s. 10 (1959) 173–8.

Southall, Raymond. *The Courtly Maker.* Oxford 1964.

Spenser, Edmund. *The Works of Edmund Spenser: a Variorum Edition.* Ed. E. Greenlaw et al. 11 vols. Baltimore 1932–57.

Stahl, W. H. *See* s.v. Macrobius.

Starnes, Dewitt T. and Talbert, Ernest William. *Classical Myth and Legend in Renaissance Dictionaries.* Chapel Hill, N.C. 1955.

Stein, Arnold. 'Wyatt's *They flee from me'. Sewanee Review* 67 (1959) 28–44.

Stevens, John. *Music and Poetry in the Early Tudor Court.* 1961.

Summerson, Sir John. *Architecture in Britain 1530 to 1830.* Harmondsworth 1953.

—'The Building of Theobalds, 1564–1585'. *Archaeologia* 97 (1959) 107–26.

Surrey, Henry Howard, Earl of. *Poems.* Ed. Emrys Jones. Oxford 1964.

Swinburne, H. *A Treatise of Spousals or Matrimonial Contracts.* 1686.

Sylvester, Joshua. *See* s.v. Du Bartas.

Talbert, Ernest William. *See* s.v. Starnes, DeWitt T.

Tatlock, J. S. P. 'Ariadne's Crown'. *Modern Language Notes* 29 (1914) 100–1.

Tervarent, Guy de. *Attributs et symboles dans l'art profane 1450–1600.* Travaux d'humanisme et renaissance 29. Geneva 1958 and 1964.

Thomson, Patricia. *Sir Thomas Wyatt and His Background.* 1964.

—*See* Muir, Kenneth, and Thomson, Patricia.

Thorndike, Lynn. *See* s.v. Sacrobosco.

Tilley, Morris Palmer. *A Dictionary of the Proverbs in England in the Sixteenth and Seventeenth Centuries.* Ann Arbor, Mich. 1950.

Bibliography

Tottel's Miscellany i.e. *Songs and sonnets, written by the right honourable Lord Henry Haward late Earl of Surrey, and other.* 1557.

Trojel, E. *See* s.v. Andreas Capellanus.

Tuve, Rosemond. *Elizabethan and Metaphysical Imagery: Renaissance Poetic and Twentieth-Century Critics.* Chicago 1947.

—*Allegorical Imagery: Some Mediaeval Books and Their Posterity.* Ed. T.P.Roche Jr. Princeton, N.J. 1966.

Tyard, Pontus de. *Oeuvres poétiques complètes.* Ed. John C. Lapp. Société des textes français modernes. Paris 1966.

Valeriano, Pierio. *Hieroglyphica ... commentariorum libri lviii. ... Accesserunt loco auctarii, hieroglyphicorum collectanea, ex veteribus et recentioribus auctoribus descripta, et in sex libros digesta.* Frankfurt 1614.

Variorum Spenser. See Spenser, Edmund.

Waller, A.R. *See* s.v. Cowley, Abraham.

Wallis, R.T. *Neoplatonism.* 1972

Walker, Alice. *See* s.v. Puttenham, George.

Willcock, Gladys D. *See* s.v. Puttenham, George.

Williams, Raymond. *The Country and the City.* 1973.

Wilson, F.P. *See* s.v. *Oxford Dictionary of English Proverbs, The.*

Wilson, Gayle Edward. 'Jonson's Use of the Bible and the Great Chain of Being in *To Penshurst'. Studies in English Literature* 8 (Houston, Texas 1968) 77–89.

Wind, Edgar. *Pagan Mysteries in the Renaissance.* New and enlarged edn 1968.

Winternitz, Emanuel. *Musical Instruments and their Symbolism in Western Art.* 1967.

Woodward, Daniel H. 'Some Themes in Spenser's *Prothalamion'. Journal of English Literary History* 29 (1962) 34–46.

Würtenberger, Franzsepp. *Mannerism: the European Style of the Sixteenth Century.* Tr. Michael Heron. New York, Chicago and San Francisco 1963.

Wyatt, Sir Thomas. *See* s.v. Muir, Kenneth and Thomson, Patricia.

Yates, Frances A. 'The Emblematic Conceit In Giordano Bruno's *De gli eroici furori* and in the Elizabethan Sonnet Sequences'. *Journal of the Warburg Institute* 6 (1943) 101–21.

Index